True Holiness:
The Wesleyan-Arminian Emphasis

Previously Published As
**True Holiness
The Arminian Emphases**
Vol. I

Schmul Publishing Co., Inc.
Wesleyan Book Club 1985 Salem, Ohio

Roy S. Nicholson

Printed by
Old Paths Tract Society Inc.
Shoals, Indiana 47581

Contents

CHAPTER		PAGE
ONE	True Holiness: A Valid Theology	13
TWO	True Holiness: Its Philosophy	21
THREE	True Holiness: Its Scriptural Basis	34
FOUR	True Holiness: Its Crisis Aspects	47
FIVE	True Holiness: Its Progressive Aspects	64
SIX	True Holiness: Its Practical Aspects	83
SEVEN	True Holiness: The Supreme Motive	92
EIGHT	True Holiness: Some Duties, Difficulties, Dangers and Distinctions	103
NINE	John Wesley's Personal Experience of Christian Perfection	122

Preface

I am signally honored to be asked to write a brief introduction of the author of this series of lectures. Dr. Roy S. Nicholson served for many years as General President of the Wesleyan Methodist Church. He is presently serving as Professor of religion at Central Wesleyan College, Central, South Carolina. His versatility is shown in his services to his church in particular, and the Christian world in general. He has served as Administrator, Author, Preacher, Lecturer, and College Instructor.

Dr. Roy S. Nicholson is a man of great mental and moral stature. For many years he has been recognized as one of the best informed men in America on the life and teachings of John Wesley. Inasmuch as this lecture series was titled "THE ARMINIAN EMPHASES," it was the opinion of the Lectureship Committee that no better exponent of these great doctrines could be found.

A careful perusal of these lectures will reveal his deep spiritual insights, the breadth of his mental grasp, his invincible logic, his incisive precision to clearly define, his scholarly approach, and his great wealth of experience from which to draw. He places the holiness message in its proper focus. He clearly shows its relevancy to our day and context of life. In these days when the fine lines of doctrinal distinction are being more or less merged, and in many instances cleverly obliterated; it is very stimulating to sit at the feet of this exegete and absorb his masterful presentations. With great versatility, he sets forth the techniques and implementing these Bible doctrines into everyday life and experience.

I commend this book to all lovers of, and adherents to, the Wesleyan Arminian persuasion. I predict for it enthusiastic reception, and am deeply grateful that in the kind providence of God, Mrs. Goodman and I have had a little part in making this Lectureship available.

M. L. Goodman

Foreword to the First Edition

In beginning this study, one feels his need of the help of the Holy Spirit. Our day is characterized by a miserable inadequacy in the care to honor the Holy Spirit as He deserves. That neglect is more real than theoretical. It is hoped that the trend is due more to ignorance than to disbelief in the Holy Spirit. These deeply spiritual truths cannot be discerned without the Spirit's assistance; and if they be neglected, one's spiritual life is dwarfed and maimed.

Care must be exercised not to omit any essential element or to overemphasize any one phase of the truth at the expense of the other phases. But a proper study of True Holiness will enable us to know God and to understand His divine purposes for man. And in this study we must ever remember that true holiness is vastly superior to the currently accepted standards of life, and lifts life to a higher plane of living than they do, as well as frequently running in an opposite direction to much that is loosely called "spiritual" life.

Many today defend holiness as an ideal but make no attempt to experience it and live it. That puts them close to the border of unreality and inconsistency, for as Barry warns us: "It is a very grave thing to habituate ourselves to the expression of devotional states in the form of words, which we permit to be forms merely, and do not strive to make actual in experience." (Meditations on the Office and Work of the Holy Spirit, pages 17, 18).

One who desires to be spiritual strives not only to know God's will—the most that God requires of him—but also strives to realize the perfect life. That means that a spiritual person lives "in accordance with spiritual motive and principle. He takes the ideal of life unfolded in the New Testament as his guide." It is true that such is a high life, and the ideal of sanctity. But it is not too high. It "begins in an action of God, it is sustained by an action of God, it ends in the enjoyment of the unveiled presence of God." The call to true holiness is to that which is high, hard, and impossible if it be restricted to human power and ability. It demands (1) Depth of spiritual insight, (2) Height of spiritual aspiration, and (3) Fervor of spiritual love. But when man quests after true holiness, God comes to his rescue and makes it possible by His grace, power, and provision in man's behalf.

In this study, let us carefully and honestly explore the propositions, examine the evidences or proofs presented, discriminating between the true and the false claims and counterclaims of the various schools of thought on this question; and let us avoid reaching any conclusion founded on prejudice or misinformation. We are morally responsible for our conclusions because we consent to the processes by which they are reached, and our eternal destiny is involved in our conclusions. Therefore, we must exercise great caution on this all-important question.

Our aim in this study will be to show that:
(1) Man is obligated to serve God with his whole being: body, soul, and spirit.
(2) That to do this effectively requires the complete yielding of himself to God through the Holy Spirit that He may dwell in him and work through him.
(3) That in response to man's consecration and faith, the Holy Spirit so indwells the Christian that all his actions become "spiritualized," or "come under the control of spiritual motives."

Thus man's heart is cleansed, he is empowered by the Spirit, his senses are purified, his intellect is enlightened, and his will is directed in such a way that he is God-controlled. Whatever such a person does, whether it be the exalted acts of faith and worship or the so-called secular things of life, he does all "to the glory of God."

One feature of these lectures is the inclusion of copious quotations from the writings of many leaders in their fields. It was felt that these would be of inestimable value to students. Efforts have been made to secure the permission of copyright owners of all materials quoted which are not in the public domain. If any were overlooked, it was an inadvertence and is regretted. Our apologies are offered for such an omission. Special thanks are due to the following publishers for permission to quote from the materials indicated:

The Epworth Press: Harald Lindstrom, *Wesley and Sanctification;* E. H. Sugden, *The Standard Sermons of John Wesley,* Annotated; Thomas Coke, *New Testament Holiness*; J. Baines Atkinson, *To The Uttermost*; Thomas Cook, *New Testament Holiness.* Fleming H. Revell: G. Campbell Morgan, *Crises of the Christ.* Marshall, Morgan and Scott: J. A. Broadbelt, *Full Salvation.* Light and Hope Publications: Samuel Chadwick, *The Way of Pentecost.* Moody Press: Ruth Paxon Hood, *Life on the Highest Plane.* Light and Life Press: J. Paul Taylor, *The Music of Pentecost.* Nazarene Publishing House: James B. Chapman, *Holiness Triumphant*; J. G. Morrison, *Our Lost Estate*; D. Shelby Corlett, ed., *The Second Grace*; T. M. Anderson, *After Sanctification, What?* Dr. Harold Paul Sloan, to quote from *Not Disobedient Unto the Heavenly Vision.*

It is acknowledged that any benefit coming from this study of true holiness is due to the gracious help and influence of the Holy Spirit, and this series of studies is sent forth with the earnest prayer that the Holy Spirit will guide all earnest seekers into the full truth about their privileges in the grace of God.

Roy S. Nicholson

Foreword to the Revised Edition

The material in this edition of the book is essentially the same as that in the first edition, except Chapter Eight which has been rewritten. The chapter divisions have been rearranged and renumbered. The material in Chapter Nine, relating to John Wesley's personal profession of Christian Perfection, has been carefully rechecked and rearranged. It originally appeared in the *Asbury Seminarian,* Wilmore, Ky., and is used by permission.

The material appearing in this volume has been used in Camp Meetings and Conventions, Seminars and Lecture Series at Seminaries at home and abroad, particularly in Japan and Korea. They were incorporated in a Japanese edition sponsored by the Immanuel General Mission of Tokyo, Japan.

Immediately following the delivery of these messages during "Holiness Emphasis Week" at Asbury Theological Seminary, Wilmore, Ky., in the early 1950's the Reverend and Mrs. Loren Anderson (students at the Seminary) in response to requests for copies, mimeographed them and bound them in a soft cover under the title: "Notes on True Holiness." In that form, two editions were circulated. Since then, they have been delivered in whole, or in part, at a number of Colleges, Bible Colleges and Seminaries under the sponsorship of their "lecture series."

The first printed edition was by Owosso College, Owosso, Mich. (Dr. Paul F. Elliott, President), under the sponsorship of the M. L. Goodman Lecture Series. Almost a decade in the classroom with theological students revealed the need of help in understanding and presenting the Wesleyan-Arminian position on Bible Holiness. One referred to it as a contest between "human cranktification" and "entire sanctification." One aim in these studies has been to use a minimum of contemporary theological terms. True holiness is of vital concern to each Christian. It is a doctrine, but it is more than that. It is an experience, but it is more than that. It is a daily life of beauty and blessing.

Such a life calls for a proper blending of doctrine, experience and life. To that end there are copious quotations from the "saints" and the "scholars" who helped to create the spiritual vitality which made the Holiness Movement a powerful force for world evangelism and moral and spiritual reform. Our prayer is: "O God, do it again!"

If there are inaccuracies in quotations or matters of proper credit, our apology is extended for each such instance. It is a matter of "infirmity" and not of "intent." Such errors will be corrected in future editions.

A word of special thanks is due to Miss Winifred R. Bisbing, a skilled secretary living in Cedar Falls, Iowa, who has given many years of sacrificial service to Christ and the Church. Miss Bisbing, now retired, volunteered to type the entire copy for this revised edition of the book. May the Lord reward her!

Our prayer is that this book will produce spiritual fruit to "the praise of His glory."

        Roy S. Nicholson

High Point, N.C.
1985

CHAPTER ONE

True Holiness: A Valid Theology

The thesis of these Studies is that true holiness is "a valid theology for our day." And it is our firm conviction that this position is supported by the Holy Scriptures, philosophy and credible human testimony. As these Studies are developed, several supporting phases will be treated, but the following are some of the bases on which we shall ground our teachings:

The Nature and Will of God. God is holy. His will is the revelation of His character. And His character is the standard for His children—which standard is to be realized in this life, as expressed in the oft-repeated divine command: "Be ye holy, for I am holy" (1 Peter 1:16). See also I Thess. 4:3, 7. The holiness of God will not permit Him to be satisfied with less than holiness in man, the acme of His creation. (Matt. 5:8, 48; Hebrews 12:14)

Humanity Needs Holiness. There is something in man which God did not put there; that is, enmity against what God is and desires for man (Romans 8:7, 8; Psalm 51:5, 7, 10). The fruitage of this enmity is described in Galatians 5:19-21. But there is also a yearning in man's heart for full deliverance from this infection of his nature. And if this God-implanted desire for deliverance be impossible of realization, it is mockery of the greatest degree, for man at his highest and best self believes that it is of God and that the nearer he draws to God, the stronger is the desire to be rid of this nature which is so unlike God.

Reason Supports the Fact That There Must Be Full Deliverance From Sin. Isaiah 1:18 is God's challenge to man to reason with Him about this matter of deliverance from the stain of sin. If man should reason with himself, or with other fallen mortals, it might seem too good to be true —or too great to be realized—that the sinful nature could be so completely removed, but God reveals that by His gracious provisions and divine power, it is gloriously possible.

Sin is basically and fundamentally an inward condition which manifests itself by outward acts. To be delivered from sin is to have the heart cleansed from the pollution, or defilement, by sin. Holiness touches "the inner recesses of the self" wherein lie the roots of human relationships, unmended divine relationships and personal defeat. It answers the need of the human personality and provides a sound basis upon which that personality can live in health.

"This belief is sound philosophically. The Universe demands moral purity and moral perfections. It demands for human personality, a purpose, 'the highest good,' a 'way of life,' and the possibility of achieving happiness."[1]

Let us consider the argument from reason thus: The religion of Jesus Christ is supernatural. Since it is supernatural, it saves from all sin. If it does not save from all sin, it is a sinning religion. But a sinning religion is ridiculous, because it represents God as pleased with sin. If God is pleased with sin, then He is not holy. Thus to deny that one can be saved from all sin is to attack the holiness of God. Therefore, we conclude with Dr. G. A. McLaughlin, that "a sinning religion is . . . a contradiction of a holy God."[2]

God's Word Teaches That Salvation From All Sin Is Provided and Possible. This truth will be especially dealt with in a subsequent Study, but for the present make a note of these Scriptures and ponder them seriously: Ephesians 1:4; 4:22-24; 5:25, 26; Romans 6:6; 1 John 1:7, 9; 3:8 and II Timothy 2:21.

The Provision of Deity Corroborates This Truth. The fact that the Trinity is involved in providing full salvation, deliverance from both the power and the pollution of sin, guarantees its realization and obligates us to faith, obedience and complete identification with God through Christ (John 3:16; Matthew 3:11; Acts 15:8, 9; I Peter 1:2; and II Thess. 2:13).

Necessity Demands Such A Doctrine, Experience and Life. Full Salvation is concerned with the inner cause of the outward symptoms of sin, the cause of all of humanity's troubles. Man finds it easier to deal with symptoms than with the cause. But the only satisfactory answer to man's need of an "inward moral dynamic to achieve personal righteousness" is the fullness of the Holy Spirit in His heart-cleansing power.

"*Human Experience Validates This Truth.*" There are thousands whose testimony is indisputable and who can exclaim: "Eureka!" "I have found it!" And their lives declare beyond a peradventure: "It works!" Holiness is practicable. Those who have it may know it; and if they have it and know it, they will show it by the "fruit of the Spirit" in their lives (Gal. 5:22, 23). And while those on earth humbly witness to the cleansing power of God, a great cloud of witnesses look down from their place of heavenly reward and shout "Amen!"

How This Doctrine Is Defined

Before we proceed farther, let us turn to some of the Churches' Manuals or Disciplines and see how this which we believe to be "a valid theology for our day" has been defined and described. Perhaps two will be sufficient for present purposes. Let us turn first to the Pilgrim Holiness Church Manual where we read:

"Entire Sanctification"

"Entire Sanctification is subsequent to regeneration (John 17:9-17) and is effected by the Baptism of the Holy Spirit (Luke 3:16, 17; I Peter 1:2; Romans 15:16). It is for all believers (John 17:20; I Thess. 4:3, 7; 5:23, 24), and it is an instantaneous experience received by faith (Acts 2:1-4; 15:8,9). It cleanses the heart of the recipient from all sin (I John 1:7, 9; Acts 15:8, 9), sets him apart, and endows him with power for the accomplishment of all to which he is called (Luke 24:49; Acts 1:8)."[3]

The Wesleyan Methodist Church speaks thus in its Articles of Religion:

"Entire Sanctification"

"Entire sanctification is that work of the Holy Spirit by which the child of God is cleansed from all inbred sin through faith in Jesus Christ. It is subsequent to regeneration, and is wrought when the believer presents himself a living sacrifice, holy, and acceptable to God, and is thus enabled through grace to love God with all the heart and to walk in His holy commandments blameless."[4]

Many years ago the Wesleyan Methodist Church adopted an "Interpretation" of this doctrine as "Appendix A," "The Reaffirmation of the Doctrines of Our Faith":

"We reaffirm our faith in the doctrine of entire sanctification, by which work of grace the heart is cleansed by the Holy Spirit from all inbred sin through faith in Jesus Christ when the believer presents himself a living sacrifice, holy and acceptable unto God, and is enabled, through grace, to love God with all his heart and to walk in His holy commandments blameless. By the act of cleansing, it is to be interpreted and taught by the ministry and teachers that it is not a 'supression' or a 'counteraction' of 'inbred sin' so as to 'make it inoperative,' but 'to destroy' or 'to eradicate' from the heart so that the believer not only has a right to heaven, but is so conformed to God's nature that he will enjoy God and heaven forever. These terms are what we hold that cleansing from all sin implies."[5]

Facing Questioners and Objectors

As surely as one begins to teach the possibility of full salvation as a personal experience to be obtained in this life, he faces those who raise questions and interpose objections. One of the questions asked is: "Can God sanctify the soul entirely in this life?" The answer is found in Paul's reference to the ability of God "to do exceeding abundantly above all that we ask or think, according to the power that worketh in us" (Ephesians 3:20). Another question is: "Will God entirely sanctify the soul in this life?" And again the Scripture replies: "This is the will of God, even your sanctification. . . . God hath not called us unto uncleanness, but unto holiness" (I Thess. 4:3, 7). The third question is: "Does God sanctify entirely here and now?" Once more the Scripture gives the answer, when incident to Paul's prayer for the Thessalonians' entire sanctification and blameless preservation, he declares: "Faithful is he that calleth you, who also will do it" (I Thess. 5:23, 24). See also I John 1:7, 9).

Those who oppose holiness may be said to do so from one of three causes: ignorance, prejudice, or unbelief. If they oppose it out of ignorance, they need to be instructed as to what sin is and does, and as to what holiness is and does. If they oppose it out of prejudice against it by reason of some inconsistent professor of the experience, or someone who wrested the Scriptures so as to teach what God never intended, they need to be persuaded by positive proof and consistent demonstration of the life of holiness. If they oppose holiness out of unbelief, it is proof that they "love darkness rather than light, because their deeds are evil." Such objectors need to be convicted by the power of the Holy Spirit as to the exceeding sinfulness of sin and the beauty of true holiness.

But when one discovers that there are objectors to holiness, who, knowing what both sin and holiness are and do, continue to prefer sin to holiness, he must recognize that such persons are evil teachers who are not to be followed. They are deceivers whose end is destruction. To follow them is to imperil the soul and expose it to eternal damnation.

A proper study of true holiness involves an investigation of man's Creation, Degeneration, and Salvation. We shall endeavor to ascertain how man was created and how he is now; why man is not as he was created; what God proposes to do for man; why God proposes to do it; how He proposes to accomplish it; and what this purpose and provision involves on the part of both God and man; how this divine purpose may be realized and demonstrated; and why its realization is necessary.

Some Definite "Problem" Areas

One cannot proceed very far in the consideration of true holiness until he perceives that there are some perplexing questions encountered, which require a solution that is scriptural and reasonable. It will be impossible to deal with all of these in the time at our disposal. But we shall indicate some of the questions which are most pertinent and on which we shall endeavor to offer help.

One problem is whether this is an imputed or an imparted holiness. Is it positional or personal?

Another problem concerns obtaining this experience.

Is it a progressive experience reached through a process of growth, or is it a crisis experience received through faith?

Again, there is the problem of the relation of holiness and the human element. How can a finite, fallen creature, subject to limitations, live a holy life in an unholy environment?

Furthermore, there are problems due to the use of varied terminology, diverse individual temperaments, and varying degrees of comprehension of this blessed truth.

There are also problems due to the imbalance between the emotions and the ethics of some who profess holiness.

There are also questions concerning its necessity and the correct motive for seeking it.

Finally, there are problems connected with certain Scriptures which some say refute the Wesleyan-Arminian position regarding holiness.

Despite the problems—real or superficial—it is our conviction that this study of true holiness will convince the honest seeker after truth that:

Holiness is likeness to God. It is what God is.

Holiness is likeness to Christ.

Holiness is not only separation from sin, but separation unto God.

It is distinctive separation: "Priestly separation for priestly service."

Holiness is God's will for every Christian.

Holiness in man is derived from God.

All holiness in man is relative.

Holiness is conditional and holiness is attainable in this life.

Facing the Difficulties Realistically

Dare we present the truth of holiness in view of the problems, difficulties and objections encountered in its presentation?

There is no need to be stampeded into panic or intimidated into silence over the fact that we encounter them. But there are some observations that apply to all Bible truths and which are pertinent to this truth:

We are to expect difficulties. We finite creatures are

endeavoring to understand and teach that which has been revealed by the Infinite God.

Difficulties in a doctrine, or objections against it, do not necessarily prove it to be untrue.

There are as many and as great—or more and greater—difficulties involved in the teachings of those who dispute the Wesleyan-Arminian teaching on holiness than in the position of those who defend it.

The fact that we cannot solve a difficulty to our own or another's satisfaction does not mean that it cannot be solved, or that the objection cannot be answered.

Most of the difficulties disappear when they are carefully and prayerfully considered and are conscientiously compared with the whole teaching of the Bible on the subject.

Some Sources of Difficulty

One problem is due to the fact that our Bible is a translation—and as such, it is exceedingly difficult for it to be properly understood in another than its original language.

Other difficulties arise out of men's varied interpretations of a truth. Many of these arise from man's preference for that which pleases him, rather than that which challenges him to a higher and separated life. Bacon said: "What a man had rather were true, he the more readily believes."

Difficulty is also due to our lack of a proper understanding of the usages of Bible times; and of the conditions which evoked the original commands.

Again, difficulty arises out of the necessity of our using words having a material connotation in order to express spiritual truth. Our very words often complicate the thoughts we seek to communicate.

Doubtless the greatest difficulty arises out of what Dr. R. A. Torrey called "the dullness of our spiritual perceptions."

All of these difficulties arise out of our own imperfection, not out of the truth concerning holiness.

Perplexing and distressing as these difficulties are, they can be solved if they be dealt with honestly, determinedly, humbly, fearlessly, patiently, scripturally, and prayerfully.[6]

Intellectual honesty will lead one in the direction of true holiness. It reveals the reality, the possibility, and the practicality of holiness.

Reason is not alone a sufficient basis for doctrine, but when coupled with Divine Revelation, it produces a binding obligation to accept the truth.

When man is confronted with the imperative which Christ issued in Matthew 5:48, he reacts in a variety of ways. One is by legalism—trying to make himself holy by what he does, or keeps himself from doing. That can lead to the strongest type of Asceticism.

Another reaction is by Antinomianism, which is an effort to escape from the dilemma of a false legalism. Man thus tries to escape "a personal responsibility of which he cannot rid himself"; and as John Knox has written, Antinomianism is an attempt "to escape from a problem which he cannot solve."[7]

What we need to recognize is that God's requirement for us to be holy is the demand of a personal, holy God upon our moral life; and that this demand "Is consistent with His nature and with the nature of His relations with me and with His creation. . . ."[8]

The obligation to be holy is inescapable. Kenneth Scott Latourette wrote: "There is that in the Christian Gospel which stirs the conscience of men to be ill content with anything short of full conformity with the ethical standards set forth in the teachings of Jesus and with the hope and the faith that, seemingly impossible of attainment though they are, progress towards them can be made and that they must be sought in communities of those who have committed themselves fully to the Christian ideal."[9]

Thus we close this study as we opened it, with the affirmation that it is our sincere belief that the doctrine of entire sanctification, or true holiness, is a valid theology of our day.

Chapter Two

True Holiness: Its Philosophy

The teaching concerning True Holiness "must be conserved and, as far as possible, rescued from the abuses to which it has become subjected. The odium which gathers about it by evil association is no excuse for its desertion. Christ, if on the gibbet, is still Christ. A jewel is still a jewel, however incrusted with base alloys. The alloys may hide the precious gem or disfigure its beauty, but cannot destroy its value. It is the task of Christian patience to remove the debasing incrustations and set it in position.

"The truth to be preserved is that there is a higher experience possible to Christians than that which is attained in and at the time of regeneration; and this must be so taught as not to reflect discredit on regeneration on the one hand or excite fanaticism on the other hand, and so as to inspire aspiration after it as duty and privilege. The possibility of enlargement is beyond question. The duty is plain. The desire is felt by every truly regenerated soul," declared Bishop R. S. Foster.[1]

This higher experience we have comprehended under the title True Holiness to distinguish it from false holiness. We propose to consider it as (1) a Bible doctrine to be believed; (2) a personal experience to be realized; and (3) a practical life to be demonstrated. Our studies will deal with this subject as follows:

    I. True Holiness: Its Philosophy
   II. True Holiness: Its Scriptural Basis
  III. True Holiness: Its Crisis Aspects
  IV. True Holiness: Its Progressive Aspects
   V. True Holiness: Its Practical Aspects
  VI. True Holiness: Some Necessary Distinctions
 VII. True Holiness: The Supreme Motive
VIII. John Wesley's Personal Experience of Christian Perfection

As a focal point let us attend to Paul's expression in the Epistle to the Ephesians 4:24, which in the King James Version reads: "And that ye put on the new man, which after God is created in righteousness and true holiness."

Let us pause to consider some of the translations which reveal man's efforts to interpret Paul's words:

The A.S.V.: "Put on the new man, that after God hath been created in righteousness and holiness of truth."

Ferrar Fenton: "The new Man, the one created Godlike in righteousness and holiness of truth."

Goodspeed: "Put on the new self which has been created in likeness to God, with all the uprightness and holiness that belong to the truth."

Weymouth: "Clothe yourselves with that new and better self which has been created to resemble God in the righteousness and holiness of the truth."

Stevens: "Giving up the old sinful life, with its corruptions, and the living of a new, inward, spiritual, holy life. Renounce, then, the sins which marked the former evil life."

True Holiness: Its Philosophy

In this treatment of our subject, it is proposed simply to give "a sufficiently full statement of the facts and contents of the subject, and furnish a rational, that is, an intelligible and adequate, explanation of it." We consider that a proper definition of the subject, with an accurate description of its nature, a statement of its cause, by what power it is produced, and a clear conception of its aim or chief end will be sufficient. As a first step, let us seek definitions from the dictionaries. One must remember that the words we shall use are but symbols used to describe a moral condition. And one must keep in mind that true holiness is a moral quality.

Webster's Unabridged Dictionary (2nd Edition, 1947) defines holiness as "1. State or character of being holy; sanctity; saintliness; consecration." Syn. . . . "Holiness suggests more frequently inherent or intrinsic state or quality." And the citation is: "Who is like unto Thee, glorious in holiness?" Sanctify: "1. To make sacred or holy . . . 2. To make free from sin; to cleanse from all moral corruption and pollution; to purify." And the quotation cited is: "Sanctify them through thy truth."

The American College Dictionary says of holiness: "The state or quality of being holy; sanctity . . . Syn. 1. godliness; saintliness; piety; sacredness." And concerning the word Sanctify: "1. To make holy; set apart as sacred; consecrate. 2. To purify or free from sin. Sanctify your hearts . . ." There seems little need to quote more of the lexicographers whose opinions are identical with the two given.

Perhaps lengthy, formal definitions which are quoted in current textbooks on theology are not necessary. Permit some corroborative definitions and explanations from theologians of another day, some of whom were not of the Wesleyan-Arminian school of interpretation. Dr. W. Newton Clarke (quoted by Dr. H. Orton Wiley): "Holiness: glorious fullness of God's moral excellence held as a principle of His own actions and standard for His creatures."

Holiness is the divine antidote for sin. As a divine attribute, holiness is purity, and purity is essential to the Being of God. . . . Applied to man, holiness means moral purity. "To be holy means to be free from sin. . . . Holiness means to be free both from the guilt and the defilement of sin. . . . Holiness implies soul normalcy. . . . Holiness is to the soul what health is to the body. . . . It is separation from sin and participation of God's purity through the indwelling Holy Spirit."[3]

"Holiness is that habitual disposition of the soul which directly implies being cleansed from all sin; from all filthiness of the flesh and spirit; and in consequence, the being endued with those virtues which were also in Jesus Christ, and being so renewed in the spirit of your minds as to be perfect even as your Father in heaven is perfect."[4]

Mr. Wesley asked, "What is holiness, according to the oracles of God? Not a bare, external religion, a round of outward duties, how many so ever they be, and how exactly so ever performed. No: gospel holiness is no less than the image of God stamped upon the heart; it is no other than the whole mind which was in Christ Jesus; it consists of all heavenly affections and tempers mingled together in one."[5]

Adam Clarke says that many who speak of what Christ

has done for us, have little to say about what He does in us. His conception of true holiness is "the restoration of man to the state of holiness from which he fell, by creating him anew in Christ Jesus, and restoring to him that image and likeness of God which he has lost. A higher meaning than this it cannot have; a lower meaning it must not have."[6] He further declares, "The object of all God's promises and dispensations was to bring fallen man back to the image of God, which he had lost. This, indeed, is the sum and substance of the religion of Christ."[7] Clarke also says that it is "fitness . . . to appear before God, and thorough preparation for eternal glory" and that it implies the pardon of all transgression and the removal of the whole body of sin and death. This must take place before we are fit to appear before God and are prepared to enjoy eternal glory.

Dr. J. G. Morrison: "Holiness is a necessity to any follower of Jesus Christ. It is the only thing that can fit one for the heavenly home wherein He dwells. It alone can equip the soul for eternal fellowship with the divine."[8]

T. K. Doty wrote: "Holiness is wholeness. It is completeness or perfection of quality and quantity. No part is lacking, and no part lacks. Nor does anything foreign to the integrity . . . inhere or adhere. It is purity, perfect and entire. . . . Holiness, therefore, belongs to the realm of the spiritual. It is purity, completion, wholeness, perfection of spiritual quality; and is shown in purity, completion, wholeness, perfection of moral action."[9]

Samuel Chadwick declared that holiness has its positive as well as its negative side, and that the holy "were to be distinguished by moral and spiritual excellence." "Holiness is an experience as well as an attitude, a life as well as a separation. Their separation unto God was to be manifest in their likeness unto Him. . . . Without holiness grace fails in its purpose, and without it no man can see the Lord. . . . Holiness is an attitude of dedication and an experience of grace in which the heart is cleansed and made perfect in love."[10]

Joseph Agar Beet says: "Holiness . . . quickens, develops, and elevates all human life. . . . Holiness not only develops, but satisfies the intelligence . . . is practicable . . . to all persons in all positions in life. . . . That holiness is possible to all men always, is some proof that the teaching which claims it, is from God.... Holiness... fits a man for every position in life.... Holiness makes us completely free from bondage to the world around, and from fear of the uncertainties and perils of life."[11]

This teaching is logical and reasonable. "The whole philosophy of the plan of salvation demands that the Christian should be made holy," that "holiness is a demand of the ethical character of God"; that "holiness is the only corrective for a sinful heart;" and that "holiness is the sum total of all the virtues." Thus, true holiness is not something optional, mythical, or freakish; it is not of the wild fire of fanaticism. When seen as God's Word reveals it, holiness is "the highest good." It means purity instead of pollution; soul health instead of spiritual unhealth; and spiritual and moral adjustment of maladjustment.[12]

It takes cognizance of what man was as God created him. It takes cognizance of what man is as sin affected him. It takes cognizance of what man may become by the grace of God.

It is not what man discovered about God, it is what God revealed to man about Himself. "I ... am holy ... Be ye holy" (I Peter 1:15, 16).

It is grounded on divine revelation—it was God Who revealed this as His will for man and as a possibility to man who needs it and yearns for it.

It agrees with human reason. Sin has a twofold aspect. It is seen as (1) A diseased state, and (2) A deliberate act.

Man's polluted nature requires cleansing, purging. His deliberate acts require forgiveness. And in Christ he has a perfect Saviour. He is able to do more than dilute the poison of sin in the soul. He is able to remove, destroy, take away that which caused the trouble—the sinful nature of man inherited from Adam. It is inconceivable that God would provide for one phase of man's spiritual need (forgiveness) and not provide for the other phase (cleansing).

It meets the requirements of right human relations: "Psychologically, holiness is the only ground for a completely integrated personality.

"Ethically, holiness is the only sound basis and possible guarantee of right relationships. Holiness is the inward, moral dynamic which enables man to achieve personal righteousness.

"Sociologically, holiness of heart is driving power to make society clean and to bring the full gospel to others."[13]

J. Baines Atkison of England declared: "The best current philosophy justifies and necessitates what is implied in the phrase, Christian Perfection." He mentions Bishop F. J. McConnell's acknowledgment that even if the words of Matthew 5:48 "were to be explained away, the command would be binding from the nature of moral insight itself."[14]

The Trinity is involved in producing true holiness in the human heart. The work of the Trinity demands and guarantees salvation from all sin.

> It is accomplished at the Father's will (Jude 1:1; I Thess. 4:3).
> It is procured through the Son's death (Eph. 5:25-27; Heb. 13).
> It is produced through the Spirit's agency (I Thess. 2:13; Matt. 3:11).

The initiative of God: Reveals His Purpose; Guarantees Its Realization; and Obligates Us to Obedience and Identification.

"On this twofold ground of the Father's will and the Saviour's work, the Holy Spirit must make real this experience in the trusting soul" (Jessop). His ministry is principally that of administering (or applying) the estate of Grace (I Cor. 1:30).

It requires a moment-by-moment dependence on Christ as Prophet, Priest and King. Mr. Wesley commented on it thus: "The holiest of men still need Christ as their Prophet, as 'the light of the world.' For He does not give them light but from moment to moment. The instant He withdraws, all is darkness. They still need Christ as their King; for God does not give them a stock of holiness. But unless they receive a supply every moment, nothing but unholiness would remain. They still need Christ as their Priest, to make atonement for their holy things. Even perfect holiness is acceptable to God only through Jesus Christ."[15]

Different Theories Concerning Holiness

It is both appropriate and necessary at this point to consider the several theories as to how one becomes the possessor of the holiness which is necessary if one is to see God (Matthew 5:8 and Hebrews 12:14). These theories reveal a difference as to time, manner and conditions. Regarding the element of time, they range from conversion to purgatory; that is, beyond death. One school of interpretation places it at conversion, others put it between conversion and death, another puts it at death, and another beyond death, in purgatory.

Also, it will be seen that some of the theories make it a gradual work, with no emphasis on any crisis aspect. Others involve a gradual approach which eventually results in an instantaneous act, even after the process of gradualism. There is another theory: that it is received by an act of faith in the provision of Christ's Atonement, and that it is available at any moment when the child of God claims it by full consecration and faith.

One of these has been called the *Conversion Theory*. More correctly, it is known as the Zinzendorfian theory. Others refer to it as the simultaneous theory. That is to say, that we are "sanctified wholly the moment we are justified, and neither more nor less holy to the day of death." This theory has been widely taught and received. But we believe that it is contrary to the Word of God, the teaching of the Early Church; and that it also "contradicts the universal consciousness of the regenerated who know that inbred sin does remain."

This theory almost proves "too much" because it involves a profession of holiness by each regenerated person, for to profess to be saved is to profess to be sanctified; and to deny sanctification is to deny a profession of saving grace. Thus, it may be said to fill the churches with members who are deceived about their conversion; or else entire sanctification is a low state of grace.

Furthermore, if this theory be true, it nullifies the many prayers, promises and promptings to holiness. And if this theory be true, these are absurd.

Another view which is as widespread as the *Conver-*

sion Theory is that of *Growth Into Holiness or Gradualism*. The heart of this teaching is that the Christian believer will eventually become holy through growth in grace. It recognizes the heart's yearning for holiness and encourages using the means of grace to pursue the quest, yet, it never allows one to realize the heart's desire for full deliverance from sin.

This is, in reality, a form of self-sanctification: It may try legalism, ritualism, asceticism; in fact, it will try almost anything to obtain holiness except the divine provision.

It holds that time is an essential element, and that by development of the spiritual life, eventually the remains of sin will be destroyed. It teaches that man can and generally does slay these inner foes one by one; and, at last, perhaps unconsciously and without any marked transition, comes into an entirely sanctified life. There is a subtle fallacy mixed up with some truth in this theory.

Of course, any dying unto sin and growth in grace bring us nearer and nearer this point of entire holiness, and are not inconsistent with a more instantaneous work. Growth in grace is to be encouraged, and may be the preliminary preparation for the act of faith which completes the work.

But, as the theory is popularly held, it antagonizes an instantaneous work, with eternally dangerous results.

Gradualism of necessity postpones and delays the work of entire sanctification. How gradual? With what rapidity may we be sanctified? Is time a necessary factor in the work? Is not gradualism an excuse for slowness, delay and unbelief? Does it not turn us away from the cleansing fountain and encourage delay?

The tendency of gradualism is to make growth a necessary condition of sanctification, when, in fact and according to the Scriptures, sanctification precedes true progress in spirituality and usefulness. Sanctification is a condition of growth—the removal of the hindrance to growth—and not growth as a necessary condition of sanctification. Gradualism reverses God's order.

It would make the death of sin depend on the vitality and growth of the spiritual nature when the Bible and experience both place the death of sin first. The development of the new life is in ratio to the death of the old. The death of sin is placed first.

A very popular theory is the *Repressive Theory*. It is spoken of variously as the *Victorious Life Theory,* the *Suppression Theory,* or the *Counter-action Theory*. Those who advocate this theory stress the need and possibility of keeping the spiritual life in the ascendancy, and keeping sin in subjection. They stress the victorious life of the believer.

But, in dealing with the sin which pollutes the heart, the fountain of moral action, they feel that sin is too deeply imbedded to be removed in this life: the virus must remain. Nevertheless, they feel that by divine aid they may suppress the foe and overcome. But in the final analysis they forget that inherited depravity cannot always be repressed or suppressed. Joe Brice declares that inbred sin may express itself "through the conceits of virtue as well as the deceits of vice."

G. Campbell Morgan wrote: "Suppression of sin is still sin, because it recognizes the presence of a principle antagonistic to God and excuses it."[17]

There are those who consider that the teaching of the destruction of sin is too rigid; and that the teaching concerning suppression is inconsistent. Therefore, they seek neutral ground by denying removal, destruction or suppression. They teach counteraction, or nullification. Nevertheless, however sincere the advocates of the various phases of this theory may be, there are some undesirable outcomes which logically follow such teaching. Let us face the facts about this theory:

It limits the power of grace. If sin can be subdued, why can it not be destroyed? Can there not be sovereignty or supremacy in the realm of the Spirit which would reduce the antagonism to nonentity or practical death?

It concentrates all attention and effort on this culprit of the lower nature, which is a waste of time and energy. "Slay the enemy within and let the guards do active duty. Instead of watching a prisoner, they can sow the fields and reap the harvests."

It can never bring a sense of safety as long as there is an evil ally in the heart who needs constant watching. "He might open the gates to the outside foe; hence, there can be no repose."

The *Imputation Theory* needs to have a word said about it. This has been called, by some, the "holy-in-Christ" theory. There is some truth in this teaching (I Cor. 1:30), but like other truths, it has been abused. It has led many into rank Antinomianism, or spiritual lawlessness. One of its really perilous aspects is that it overlooks or ignores personal responsibility and personal character. Although we receive nothing except what we receive through Christ's Atonement, this theory produces no real deliverance from sin. Instead, it leaves one to struggle with the conflict between "the two natures." This school of interpretation stresses holiness by "standing." Some of its advocates have said that our condition "in Christ" is like a barnyard under a blanket of snow. The sin and ugliness are there, but between us and God is the snowy whiteness of Christ's righteousness which is imputed to us. That seemed logical enough for a moment, but there was no answer to the question: "What happens when it thaws?"

The next theory is called the *Dying Grace Theory,* or the *Death-of-the-Body Theory*. Some have called this "the Protestant theory" to distinguish it from the Catholic theory of purgatory. Generally speaking, this "death" theory, however expressed, is associated with the Calvinistic school of interpretation. In brief, it teaches that we are not—and indeed cannot be—sanctified entirely until death. Some have expressed its effect as one's being made holy "in the hour and article of death." But those who advocate this theory cannot deny that "God in sovereign righteousness" can cut the work short and sanctify the soul fully before death.

The fallacy of this theory is that it makes the "body the seat of sin, and revives that old exploded philosophy that matter is necessarily evil." This retains traces of the Gnostic heresy, a heresy which St. John attacked and repudiated in his First Epistle. This theory makes death do for us what it denies that Christ's death can do for us. By thus making death a necessary agent in man's redemption from sin, it detracts from the power of Christ's Atonement, "making the work of death supplement its failures."

Before we pass to the next theory, let us pause to consider the errors in this "sanctified-by-death" teaching:

> It annuls the force of all the Scriptures which make holiness a means to an end, and connect it with subsequent acts and habits to be exhibited by the believer during life and before death.
>
> It would argue the possibility of an instantaneous sanctification. "If instantaneous . . . in the dying hour, why not now in the living hour?" If it be a sovereign act of God when man dies, the continuance in sin might be chargeable to God—hence man has a part to perform.
>
> "If faith on the part of man is a condition, and the Atonement is the agent of sanctification, we can leave death out of the process, and come to the cleansing fountain."

The *Catholic Theory* of sanctification has some things in common with several of the other theories. Dr. Paul S. Rees[18] spoke of this phase of teaching as calling for "segregations, scourgings, midnight vigils, macerations . . ." in this life. Nor is that all, as is well known. There is more required after death. Thus has this view come to be referred to as the "post-mortem" theory. The purifying of the soul is made to depend upon the fires of "purgatory." This human invention is plainly a wresting of the Scriptures. Instead of an extended reply to this heretical theory, suffice it to say that one who loves the truth prefers to be purged by God Himself (John 15:2).

The last of the theories which we shall mention is the *Faith Theory of Instantaneous Sanctification*. "Notwithstanding the repressive power of the Spirit-life, the growth of the divine principle, and the gradual approach toward the realization of entire sanctification as preliminary, though not necessary operations, we hold that there comes a point, somewhere between conversion and the dying hour, when the Christian is wholly sanctified, and that faith determines that point. It may be one minute before dying—it may be one minute after conversion—it may be now. In the nature of things, and according to the Word of God, it must be before dying and after conversion, and by a special act of faith in the fullness and cleansing power of the atonement. If by faith, it may be now.

"The mode of its accomplishment may vary according to the education, temperament and light of the Christian. The special manifestations of the blessing and power may be different with different individuals—the time of the transition may not be so marked and definite in all cases—but the fact of the transition, and the accomplished work, is a matter of consciousness and experience, demonstrated by the subsequent holy life."[19]

These are the leading theories among evangelical Christians on this subject. They more or less blend and have some points in common; yet differ in some essential features and authorize us to make these distinctions.

The Faith Theory is the True Theory

It runs alongside each of the others; and at length towers above them, and we crown it as an experiential fact. The others come short of a real experience and life. "The Faith Theory runs along with the others, until they reach the clouds. There they stop, but faith penetrates the clouds and finds the sunshine of an accomplished fact in the experience of the believer. The Faith Theory cannot be left out. If so, there is a want in the other theories. But you can tear down these other shorter columns and leave this one, and, like a shaft of gold, it rests its foot on the cross and has its apex above the stars, crowned with a diadem of glory."

Its relation to the other theories has been so well described by another that we quote his own words:

"It comes to your Zinzendorf Theory and tells the regenerated soul, who is conscious of inbred sin, though compelled by its logic to profess holiness—there is nothing to hinder you from another plunge into the cleansing stream; in fact, you had better stay under the blood.

"To the Dying Grace Theory, it says: 'You may have living grace, and that is better still. You may have the advantage of this grace in the trials and toils of human life, a power for good while living, and a pillow of peace when dying.'

"To the Repressive Theory, it says: 'I will exterminate the foes and slay the body of sin; then your guards which have done nothing but watch the old prisoner, may go forth and sow fields and gather harvests.'

"To the Gradual Theory, it says, 'For forty long years you have been going in a circuitous route, often in sight of the promised land of perfect love and rest, why not go up at once and possess the land, for ye are well able? The wilderness life need not be so long. Canaan is near. Only the narrow Jordan of unbelief rolls between.' "[20]

May God help us to know the truth, and knowing the truth, be set free from all sin in all its nature and manifestations.

In our next study, God willing, we shall consider the Scripture Basis for our teaching on true holiness. But in the meantime, keep in mind that the holiness which we advocate is: "relative to our creaturely experience and earthly limitations; derived from God's grace in Christ, not based on any merit of our own; progressive, or capable of indefinite improvement; alienable, or forfeitable; not guaranteed to perpetuity, but conditional on faith, our striving against sin, and steadfast abiding in the love of God...."[21]

In conclusion, consider this summary by evangelist, Dr. Russell V. DeLong:

"Holiness is theologically sound; theoretically reasonable; philosophically the highest good; psychologically desirable; ethically imperative; sociologically necessary; Biblically commanded; practically satisfying; and experientially, gloriously possible."[22]

Therefore, let us study it carefully, seek it diligently, secure it promptly, and scatter it globally.

CHAPTER THREE

True Holiness: Its Scriptural Basis

The essence of our preaching, teaching and practice is "holiness of heart and life." And it must be a fundamental in our doctrine that "the Bible is the whole and sole rule both of Christian faith and practice" as Mr. Wesley wrote in 1786: "(1) That religion is an inward principle; that it is no other than the mind that was in Christ; or, in other words, the renewal of the soul after the image of God, in righteousness and true holiness. (2) That this can never be wrought in us, but by the power of the Holy Ghost. (3) That we receive this, and every other blessing, merely for the sake of Christ: And (4) That whosoever hath the mind that was in Christ, the same is our brother, and sister, and mother."[1]

Please remember that holiness is (1) a Bible doctrine to be believed; (2) a personal experience to be realized; and (3) a practical life to be lived. And it is with the Scriptural basis of true holiness that we now deal. It is our aim to show that true holiness is "the inner condition for outward righteousness," and that it is God's only and perfect cure for sin, and an unqualified requirement for admission into heaven.

This will lead us into a consideration of the holiness of God, the holiness in man, the varied terminology used to describe this glorious teaching, and a summary of Bible statements concerning true holiness, which Bishop Merrill called "the aim of all Christian endeavor, the crown of Christian experience and the essence of Christian character and enjoyment."[2]

When commands are given to man or obligations are imposed upon him, he instinctively asks for "the authority" for such commands and obligations. To Christians the "supreme court of final appeal" is the Word of God. Beyond this there is no higher authority. In the Bible we have God revealing Himself and His will to man. This revelation implies: (1) That there is a God Who has a will to reveal to man; and (2) man's ability to receive that revelation, for God gave it to man as he was able to receive it, leading him, as one has said, "from the A.B.C. class of redemption" to the pinnacle of final revelation of the mind and purposes of God in the New Testament.

Although the experience of holiness is a very personal matter, it is not left to the individual opinion, for that would destroy the divine authority. And when man rejects the supreme, divine authority, he turns to human authorities, which are divided and divergent on vital issues. Therefore, man must be very careful lest he erroneously excoriate something or some ideal instead of examining it. Paul once did that to the Christian religion, thinking meantime, that he was doing God's will.

We must not only be intellectually awake to perceive the problems which may be presented in this study, but also we must be intellectually persevering to pursue them to their solution. Some are troubled about the Bible teaching on True Holiness because they have not made the mental exertion necessary to verify the truth by their own honest investigation. And others have been prejudiced against it by the unfounded claims and boasted authority of those who dispute the truth.

But in spite of what man says about those whom God's Word calls "holy" and those who are called to be holy — "the vocation to sanctity is the universal Christian vocation. . . . All those are called to be saints who are called to be Christians: they are not two things, but one."[3]

The Holiness of God (Exodus 15:11)

"Holiness, considered as an attribute of God, is His perfect moral purity. It is that perfection of His nature by which He is infinitely averse to all moral evil, and inclined to love all that is good and right. The holiness of God, then, implies the absence of all moral impurity and imperfection, and the possession, in an infinite degree, of all that is morally pure, lovely, and excellent."[4]

"Perfect holiness is entire moral goodness, to the exclusion of all moral evil. God is absolutely holy, because He possesses in His own nature, all possible moral good to the exclusion of every kind and degree of moral evil.... The holiness of God may ... be contemplated in a twofold view.

"1. As absolute purity, involving the absence of all moral evil or defilement ...

"2. The holiness of God is not merely negative, but positive, consists not only in the absence of all evil, but in the presence of all possible, operative goodness. ... As a sentiment or disposition, the holiness of God may be regarded as involving three things ...

"(1) An infinite hatred and opposition to sin, or moral evil of every kind and degree. Psa. 45:7; Heb. 1:9; Habakkuk 1:12, 13.

"(2) An infinite love or regard for all that is good and right and holy....

"(3) A practical exemplification, and actual communication of goodness, and diffusion of holiness and happiness, so far as is consistent with the law of right, and as can be done in harmony with all the attributes of God, which, as a whole, render Him absolutely and infinitely perfect."[5]

"Holiness is the glorious fullness of God's moral excellence, held as the principle of His own action and the standard for His creatures. In this definition are three elements, all of them important. No one of them must be overlooked ... holiness is not God's character alone, or God's self-consistency alone, or God's requirements alone. It is all three. It is His character consistently acted out by Himself, and unalterably insisted upon with us men. It is a quality of His entire Being.

"(1) God's holiness dictates the end for which He created and is conducting the universe....

"(2) Since holiness dictates God's end in the universe, it follows that for all beings who are capable of goodness, holiness, or strong and consistent goodness, is necessarily His standard: This He requires. His self-consistency must dominate His universe. He cannot have one standard for Himself and another for His creatures; hence, He requires men to be holy, and endeavors to make them so....

"(3) It follows, further, that if sin exists, holiness in God must absolutely and forever oppose it. Sin is the opposite of that moral goodness for the sake of which God created the universe; and sin tends directly to the defeat of

His holy desire and purpose. God, therefore, acting in holiness, is against it. . . .

"(4) From this view of holiness, we can understand God's justice or righteousness, which is a form of His holiness. . . .

"(5) God's holiness is thus the basis of moral significance in His universe."[6]

In the Books of the Law, we see holiness objectively as having its source in God; and subjectively as it involves man's obligation by reason of God's claims on him to be holy. And since the purpose of man's relationship to God is to glorify Him by his love and service, the moral aspect begins to emerge—for "devotion to God involves separation from all impurity."[7]

And when we pass to the New Testament, we find that those writers "perpetuate and develop the Old Testament conception of holiness."[8] But they are careful to show that separation from sin and devotion to God do not necessitate isolation from society. Sanctity never interrupts our citizenship; it enhances our value to society.

Therefore, we believe that when we speak of True Holiness as a Bible doctrine, we are on solid ground scripturally.

As a doctrine, it is "the central idea of our Christian faith."

As a doctrine, it requires intellectual assent, but more than assent is necessary.

As a doctrine, it agrees with the highest and best of human reason as well as the clearest divine revelation, as may be seen by the following quotations from Dr. Augustus H. Strong:

"There can be no proper doctrine of the Atonement, and no proper doctrine of retribution, so long as holiness is refused its pre-eminence. Love must have a norm or standard, and this norm or standard can be found only in holiness."[9]

"Holiness is purity of substance . . . purity, however, in ordinary usage is a negative term and means only freedom from stain and wrong. . . ."[10] E. G. Robinson in one of the Yale Lectures on Preaching said: "Holiness is moral purity, not only in the sense of absence from all moral stain, but of complacency in all moral good." And to quote Dr. Strong again: "Holiness is the opposite to impurity; that is, it is itself purity."[11] And Strong remarked further: "This purity . . . is not simply a passive and dead quality; it is the attribute of a personal being; it is penetrated and pervaded by will. . . . Holiness is purity willing itself. . . . The center of personality is will."[12]

Thus we see that this doctrine:
> Tells of the principle which characterizes God: "God is Holy."
> Tells of man's creation by God: "In the image of God created He him."
> Tells of man's loss of his holiness: Through the Fall in Eden. (See Gen. 3.)
> Tells of God's provision to restore man to a state of holiness: Christ is a perfect Redeemer. (Matt. 1:21; John 1:29).
> And it tells of God's eternal and immutable will for man: "Holiness without which no man shall see the Lord" (Heb. 12:14).

The Holiness in Man

The great question facing man is whether or not he can be godlike. When we speak of the holiness of God, we speak of "essential and absolute perfection"; but when we speak of holiness as it relates to men, it "denotes entire conformity to the will of God." But note:

Some men are called "holy" because of their being vessels, consecrated to God, or sustaining a peculiar relationship to Him and His cause; i.e., set apart, consecrated; or belonging to some organization dedicated to God. (Rom. 8:27; 12:13; I Cor. 6:2; Eph. 2:19; 6:18, etc.). Holiness does mean separation and consecration, but more!

Others are called "holy" because of their personal character: they are separated from sin, think and act in a godlike manner, and their inner being and outward conduct conform to the will of God. (Rom. 6:19, 22; Eph. 1:4; Titus 1:8; I Peter 1:15).

Thus holiness in man is a moral state, which is produced by God's gracious work of sanctification. Divine holiness underlies the idea of holiness in man, and apart from God's holiness, there is no possibility of holiness in man. The fact that God is holy is the reason or obligation and the ground of the possibility of holiness in man.[13]

"As the divine holiness is the reason for Christian holiness, there must be a likeness between the two," declared Wiley, who also suggested that one point of difference is that between the infinite fullness of God and the narrow limitations of man—a difference which no one can ever afford to overlook; and that another point of difference is that in God holiness is an eternal possession, "while Christian holiness is an attainment"—or is conditional.[14] Wiley's view is that "the reality of sanctification concerns us far more deeply than any question respecting the mode of the work within the soul."[15] But the mode of the work, however, is of importance.

The grounds of true holiness "according to outward appearance are twofold, viz.: (a) Holiness is given of God by the mediation of Christ, conditioned upon faith and an inward surrender (consecration) which are themselves likewise the gift of God. (b) Man from within, by a proper purification of the heart, may attain this sanctity. Although the last cannot occur without the assistance of God, yet the personal activity of man is necessary and almost preponderant. Still, even interior holiness is, as above implied, the direct work of God."[16]

True holiness beings in regeneration, as Mr. Wesley plainly taught with scriptural warrant. Bishop Merrill said: "Holiness and spiritual life are joined together if not identical. They are so related that one does not exist without the other." He further declared: "Holiness is freedom from sin. In those once subject to sin and defiled by sin, it implies the destruction of the reigning power of sin, and the washing away of all its pollution."[17]

There are definite limitations to holiness in man:
It is not Absolute—only God is thus.
It is not Adamic—that is not for us.
It is not Angelic—that does not concern us.
It is not what we shall be in the post-resurrection state.
It is not maturity—which comes by growth.
It is not freedom from human infirmities: "We have this treasure in earthen vessels, that the excellency of the power may be of God, and not of us" (II Cor. 4:7).
It is not the destruction of any of the "constitutional" faculties, appetites, affections, and susceptibilities, for

man is all right as God "constituted" him. But it does mean the proper regulation and control of all these things. This is not the destruction of personality; but its enhancement and its enrichment by reason of its being enriched and properly integrated through the removal of the carnal nature.

Man not only may, but must, choose to live by the standard given to him by the Holy One who created him. Deviation from God's will breaks man's fellowship with God. But that fellowship may be re-established and maintained through God's gracious provision for man to be made holy in heart and righteous in life through Jesus Christ. (See I Cor. 1:30, 31; I John 1:6, 7; 2:1-3.)

Thus the divine nature demands holiness in man. This requirement is immutable. It always was and ever will be the same: "Be ye holy, for I am holy" (I Peter 1:16). (See also II Cor. 6:17, 18; 7:1.)

Man's nature, as a consequence of the Fall, needs to be made holy. "Because the carnal mind is enmity against God: for it is not subject to the law of God, neither indeed can be" (Romans 8:7).

This introduces us to the heart of the problem: How "to get rid of sin—to change the sinner to a saint; to make him such a being as a holy God can love. So to revolutionize him that holy law can approve him, and holy beings associate with him, and holy happiness come to him. His impure thoughts must be taken out of him, his unholy nature must be changed, his rebellious will must be made loyal, his malice and selfishness must be replaced with love, he must be put into harmony with heaven's people and heaven's law, and heaven's spirit and heaven's practices. There is no other way to save him."[18]

The Design of Redemption (Hebrews 7:25; 13:12)

It is at this very point of "the double cure" for man's double need—the solving of "the world's major problem—the curing of sin's disease—the cleansing of man's nature, infected by sin—the expulsion of the usurper on the throne of men's hearts"—that we observe "the trend of redemption."

"Redemption . . . is only complete," says Dr. G. Campbell Morgan, "when man is restored to the perfection of his being, and thus to fitness for the fulfillment of the Divine purpose. This then is the ultimate issue of the work of Christ in man.... Redemption is ... the restoration of man to fellowship with the Father."[19]

Wakefield taught that "the immediate design of the atonement was to meet the claims of God's holy law; but the ultimate design was to restore men to the state of holiness from which they had fallen. The means were of the most wonderful and unexpected kind—the substitution and sufferings of a Divine person—the obedience and crucifixion of the Lord of glory. He 'gave Himself for us, that He might purify unto Himself a peculiar people, zealous of good works' (Titus 2:14). It follows, therefore, that holiness must be infinitely acceptable to God, and that He is an infinitely holy Being, since He resorted to this extraordinary method of re-establishing holiness in our world."[20]

The justice of God's redemptive plan is beyond dispute. The method by which the soul is led from sin to true holiness "violates no ethical law ... does not require the surrender of holiness on God's part and ... does not violence to the freedom of man ... it imperils no interest of the universe ... it honors eternal justice and external love. It is a process which not only may issue in salvation—that is, not only furnishes a rational ground for salvation, but on ethical principles must issue in salvation. He that was a sinner, and as such was of ethical necessity excluded from heaven, which is but another name for holy happiness, by the change through which he has passed was exactly that which was needed—the means answer to the end as any effect answers to its cause."[21]

"The whole trend of redemption aims at personal holiness." And "the primal design" is to "destroy the works of the devil" (I John 3:8).

The holiness of God is an incentive for man to be holy. "Speak unto all the congregation of the children of Israel, and say unto them, Ye shall be holy: for I the Lord your God am holy" (Lev. 19:2). "Be ye therefore perfect, even as your Father which is in heaven is perfect" (Matt. 5:48).

"In the year that King Uzziah died, I saw also the Lord sitting upon a throne, high and lifted up, and his train filled the temple.

"Above it stood the seraphims: each one had six wings; with twain he covered his face, and with twain he did fly.

"And one cried unto another, and said, Holy, holy, holy, is the Lord of hosts: the whole earth is full of his glory.

"And the posts of the door moved at the voice of him that cried, and the house was filled with smoke.

"Then said I, Woe is me! for I am undone; because I am a man of unclean lips, and I dwell in the midst of a people of unclean lips: for mine eyes have seen the King, the Lord of hosts.

"Then flew one of the seraphims unto me; having a live coal in his hand, which he had taken with the tongs from off the altar:

"And he laid it upon my mouth, and said, Lo, this hath touched thy lips; and thine iniquity is taken away, and thy sin purged" (Isaiah 6:1-7).

The "original purpose of God" was personal holiness. "According as he hath chosen us in him before the foundation of the world, that we should be holy and without blame before him in love" (Eph. 1:4). "Elect according to the foreknowledge of God the Father, through sanctification of the Spirit, unto obedience and sprinkling of the blood of Jesus Christ: Grace unto you, and peace, be multiplied" (I Peter 1:2).

The ability of God is our assurance of the possibility of true holiness. "Wherefore he is able also to save them to the uttermost that come unto God by him, seeing He ever liveth to make intercession for them" (Heb. 7:25). This much-debated passage offers definite encouragement to seekers after full deliverance from inward sin.

Mr. Wesley's comments on it are: "From all the guilt, power, root and consequence of sin."

Thayer's Lexicon says the word for "uttermost" means "completely, perfectly, utterly."

Tittmann (quoted in J. F. & B. Commentary) says: "So that nothing is wanting afterwards forever."

Dr. A. B. Davidson says that "uttermost" refers to "degree or perfection of salvation. . . . He is able to save completely, to bring them through all hindrances to that honor and glory designed for them (Heb. 3:7, 10) which He Himself had reached as the Captain of their salvation" (*Commentary on Hebrews*).

Albert Barnes considers that "to the uttermost . . ." "does not simply mean forever—but that He has the power to save them so that their salvation shall be complete. . . . He can aid us as long as we need anything done for our salvation. . . ."

Adam Clarke considers that the emphasis hinges on the words: "Come unto God through Him"—"imploring mercy through Him as their sacrifice and atonement. . . ."

The faithfulness of God assures the realization of true holiness. "Faithful is he that calleth you, who also will do it" (I Thess. 5:24).

The Diversity in Terminology

Many profess to be confused by the varied terminology used to describe true holiness. Admittedly some expressions are scriptural, others are definitive, while others are figurative and describe those phases which most greatly impressed or appealed to the writers at a given time or under given circumstances.

Words are sometimes poor symbols to accurately describe moral and spiritual values and states. But beware lest the objection is really against the thing signified rather than against the terminology employed. A variety of terms is necessary because no one, or any combination of them, is able to describe the life of true holiness. One should, however, avoid becoming tied to, or prejudiced by mere terms; and especially those which are extra-Biblical.

Some speak of this as: the deeper life, the higher life, life on the highest plane, the victorious life, the surrendered life, the consecrated life, the Spirit-filled life, the fruitful life, the life of faith, the rest of faith, the life of perfect love, the sanctified life, the more abundant life, the overcoming life, and abiding grace.

Others speak of it as: the holy life, a life of purity, the fullness of the blessing, the double cure, the fullness of faith, the crucified life, the interior life, living in Beulah Land, the Canaan experience, the ideal Christian life, the

Christ-life, the spiritual life, the fulness of Pentecost, the perfect life, Christian perfection, entire sanctification, death to sin, freedom from sin, the Baptism with the Holy Spirit, the heavenly anointing, the blessing, the blessed assurance, and the inheritance among the sanctified. Even so, the list is not exhausted. Nor do all of them together exhaustively define or describe this glorious truth concerning true holiness.

True Holiness: A Summary of its Biblical Basis

It begins when one is born again; hence, it is of divine origin. (Rom. 12:13; I Cor. 1:2, 6:11; Eph. 5:3).

It is not completed in regeneration; hence, true believers yearn for a deeper experience in God's grace. (I John 15:2; 17:17; Eph. 4:22-24; I Thess. 5:23).

That such an experience is possible in this life is "the central theme of the Bible"; "the central idea of Christianity"; "the central purpose of redemption"; it is "the secret" of victorious and effective living; and it is "the inward condition for outward righteousness."

It is eternally purposed; hence, it is not a new theory (Eph. 1:4). It is not Wesleyan, not Methodist in origin, but it is Biblical—man would not and could not have conceived of such a thing. It remained for God to purpose it. It is required by God's holy law which never requires anything impossible, unnecessary, or unreasonable.

It is divinely provided; hence, it is not of human origin (Heb. 10:8-10; Eph. 5:25-27). Since it is provided by the death of Christ, it must be a necessary part of redemption's plan.

It is fully revealed; hence, any confusion or obscurity about it is due to man's ignorance, prejudice, or unbelief (Lev. 11:44; I Peter 1:15, 16; Heb. 12:14; Matt. 5:48). It is to the soul what health is to the body.

It is instantaneously wrought by the Holy Spirit, subsequent to regeneration; hence, it is a divine work of grace and is not conditioned on time or growth, but on consecration and faith (Acts 2:1-4; 19:1-6; 15:8, 9; Romans 8:32; 15:16; I Peter 1:2; II Thess. 2:13; Romans 12:1, 2).

One referred to it as "the climax of the work of the Holy Spirit in the soul."[22] Another called it "the only cure for sin."[23] It is the necessary prerequisite for holy living and effective soul winning.

It is freely offered to all; hence, it is not restricted to any select group, chosen nation, privileged minority, or particular order or sect. It is "salvation free, full and felt" (Acts 2:38, 39; Joel 2:28, 29; John 17:20).

It is complete in its scope; hence, it does not exclude any essential part of man or life (I Thess. 5:23; Col. 3:1-3, 17; Phil. 4:8). It includes the body which gives one world-consciousness; the soul which gives one self-consciousness; and the spirit which gives one God-consciousness. It is entire, "wholly"; and its moral philosophy is purity. By the keeping power of the grace of God, it is a moral preservative, "preserved blameless unto the coming of our Lord Jesus Christ."

It is reasonable in its requirements; hence, there is no excuse for man's indifference or hostility toward it. It requires:
        Consecration (Romans 12:1, 2).
        Implicit obedience (I Sam. 15:22).
        Personal, appropriating faith (Hebrews 11:6).

Our trouble is not with faith, but with the antecedents of faith.

It is beautiful in its demonstration; hence, winsom and attractive, as well as practical (I Cor. 13). In true holiness, there is nothing strained or unnatural: "As He is, so are we . . . world" (I John 4:17).

It is a conscious personal experience, amply attested by the direct witness of the Holy Spirit and by the indirect fruit of the Spirit; hence, there is no ground to doubt its reality (Romans 8:16; Heb. 10:14, 15; Gal. 5:22, 23; Matt. 7:20; I John 2:3; 5:10). Furthermore, it is abundantly corroborated by a great "cloud of witnesses."

It is the unqualified condition for admission into heaven; hence, my attitude toward it in this life determines my eternal destiny (Matt. 5:8, 48; Heb. 12:14).

It is eternal in its duration; hence, it is not a transitory experience for this life only (I Cor. 13:13; Rev. 22:11). It begins in man here, but it never ends. It is not finality, but it is fitness to appear before God and share His glory. Thus, we see that true holiness is a gracious experience "for the here and now," giving one inward fitness for "outward righteousness," making man like God through Christ's provision, and thus fitting him "to fulfill the primal divine purpose." Such a doctrine and experience, grounded on the Word of God, cannot be denied. We cannot evade our responsibility to be holy. We cannot deny that we have been furnished a satisfactory motive for, and model of, holiness (I Peter 1:15, 16; I John 4:17).

CHAPTER FOUR

True Holiness: Its Crisis Aspects

In continuing our consideration of True Holiness, we come now to consider its crisis aspects.

At the outset of our studies, we recognized there were problems connected with the study of this question. Some of them are:

> "What position does sanctification occupy in the order of divine blessings? What is the connection between regeneration and sanctification? . . . Exactly what is the place of sanctification in regard to salvation; does it precede or follow, or is it an integral part of it?"[1]

The critics of the Wesleyan-Arminian position say that the demand for holiness is the command of One Who is absolutely Holy and Perfect for man, who is imperfect, to be absolutely perfect when the demand of perfection is impossible. They try to explain away the force of the command as well as its content. But again, you are reminded that it is not *absolute* perfection for which we plead, but *relative* perfection.

Those who do this may be "self-righteous Pharisees" or "self-satisfied Laodiceans." There are some others, the Antinomians, "who cut the knot (instead of untying it) and deny all difficulty, by asserting that the holiness of Christ is imputed to us. But those who realize that God requires personal holiness, yet are conscious of their own filthiness, are deeply concerned thereupon."[2]

One of the questions asked by sincere Christians is: "How is this blessing obtained? by something which is done for us, or by us, or both?"[3]

This study will endeavor to answer some of these questions, and others will be considered later.

We believe that this experience is later than regeneration. We believe that it is distinct from, but related to, justification and glorification. We believe that it is a vital part of salvation, and that it is something provided for us, done in us and dependent upon our faith and obedience.

What Is Meant By "Crisis"?

Furthermore, we believe that it is a crisis experience which involves a cleansing of the heart.

By crisis, we mean: "a point of time when it is decided whether any affair or course of action must go on, or be modified or terminate; a decisive moment; a turning point; also a state of things in which a decisive change one way or the other is impending. . . . In medicine: That change in a disease which indicates whether the result is to be recovery or death. . . ."[4]

"In the cure of the soul, pardon is only the crisis of convalescence; the restoration of health is sanctification."[5]

There is considerable scorn thrown upon those who profess holiness, but hear what Dr. A. J. Gordon says: "If the doctrine of sinless perfection is a heresy; the doctrine of contentment with sinful imperfection is a greater heresy. It is not an edifying spectacle to see a Christian worldling throwing stones at a Christian perfectionist."[6]

Those who argue against the Wesleyan-Arminian interpretation of full salvation fallaciously reason without taking into account:

> The purpose of God
> The power of God
> The authority of God

"A partial realization on the part of a child of God of the salvation of Jesus Christ is the very thing Satan delights in, because it leaves within that one the remains of the sinful disposition . . . the carnal mind . . . which is the connection with the body of sin. . . . If this place of entire sanctification is not reached, there is always that in us which has a strong affinity with the devil, whose desire is to 'split up the personality.' "[7]

"One of the most interesting and practically important questions connected with the Divine plan of salvation is: What degree of deliverance from sin is scriptural for the believer to expect in this life?"[8]

To help us find the answer to this question, let us review the nature of sin—for sin and holiness stand in direct contrast to each other. One cannot properly appreciate salvation until he knows the truth about sin. Sin is a very personal experience; so is salvation. "God does not perfect His sons in the mass, He perfects them in the individual."

Sin is an evil inheritance, a separation from God. Sin is a disease, a state, and an act. And just as sin suggests "a sinner, an intelligent, free being, subject to a law, and responsible to a Lawgiver, a being capable of doing the wrong acts, and being in the wrong state, which sin is liable to the disorder, the alienation from God, the delusion and the doom—even so the idea of salvation implies a Saviour, a being who is able to do all that is implied in the rescue of the sinner from that doom, from that delusion, that disorder, that alienation, that evil state."[9]

Redemption Proposed and Accomplished

Salvation, therefore, to be real and complete must be viewed as an act, as a state, as healing, as a return to God, a recovery from a delusion, and the restoration of the lost moral image of God. In one word, as true holiness. Anything less than that is not full salvation. Lost man totally corrupted and impaired, needs the perfect salvation designed by God.

Through Christ, God has adequately provided for all man's spiritual need. He not only attempted the work of redemption, but "perfectly accomplished" it, "so that the sinner may more than regain the paradise from which the parents of the race were expelled; indeed, he may be renewed in the image and likeness of God; he may be delivered from the guilt and corruption and power of sin; he may be endued with power from on high; he may be adopted into the heavenly family, and so become with Jesus Christ an heir of an eternity of blessedness and glory."[10]

Such an experience is very personal. It is not a wild dream nor the fruit of a fanatical mind. It is a very real life within the divinely-revealed possibilities of grace. Such a great and personal salvation involves a crisis in the soul of the believer. It produces definite points or stages in the soul's experience when the changes are often abrupt; when both the inward nature and outward conduct are radically reversed. Regeneration is such a crisis. Entire sanctification, which results in true holiness, is such a crisis. And who can deny that glorification will also be a crisis—the consummate crisis of all crises!

In such crisis experiences, there is much to perplex one. Part of the perplexity regarding the crisis of entire sanctification grows out of the Scripture's use of "figurative forms" to represent the corruption or depravity of human nature. The same thing is true of "the forms in which the cleansing or purification of the soul is expressed. The result is that we have difficulty in grasping in clear thought the spiritual things which lie back of these physical representations." Depravity and holiness, though represented by material forms, are not "substances" within the soul: they are moral states of the soul. The "use of physical terms" cannot "exactly define purely spiritual matters."[11]

Despite the mystery which surrounds the question of "how" Almighty God removes sin from a diseased soul, it is as real as, and not more mysterious than, the fact that finite man can somehow minister to diseased fellowman and precipitate a crisis in his case which results in a cure. Sin has been described as "a virus in the bloodstream of the moral nature, a virulence, a malignancy moving within the moral nature of man." But our God by supernatural power and divine grace can remove this virulence as well as forgive man's guilt.

We now state our proposition: True Holiness is a personal experience which involves a crisis of cleansing.

We admit that the problem is not only what God does with sin, but how He does it.

We believe that our proposition is proved by "Church History, the church Creeds, church Confessions, by reason, by nature, by Scripture, and by the experience of millions of saints."[12]

This Crisis Experience Is Logical

The fall of man involved a crisis. Conversion involves a crisis. And likewise, entire sanctification which produces true holiness involves a crisis. It fits one for glorification which is a crisis of resurrection or translation.

At the point of emphasis on holiness as a crisis of cleansing, many go away and walk no more with us. Generalizing on holiness arouses very little opposition, but when specific claims are made for it as a crisis of cleansing, many become controversial. But there is nothing illogical or unscriptural about such a crisis, despite man's claims to the contrary.

Different Sense of Needs

The seeker after pardon has a different conception of his spiritual need from that of the seeker after cleansing. The seeker after pardon feels a sense of guilt for his actual transgressions, and is driven by a sense of fear; a sense of divine displeasure. He is more concerned about the consequence of his acts of sin than about his sinful nature. The sinner wants God to turn His anger away from him and love him. And he cannot know this until he is forgiven. His sins are a personal matter between him and God and the sinner's need is what drives him in fear of punishment to seek pardon.

The seeker after holiness conceives his greatest need as being for cleansing. He knows that there is a cause back of the acts of sin. He is not conscious of willing anything outside the will of God. But he finds remaining in him sinful tendencies which he is conscious would, if possible, cause him to will something outside the will of God. And he finds remaining in him this foe that needs expelling.

Different Motives

Another point of difference is that the motives of the two groups of seekers differ. The seeker after pardon was moved principally by fear, a legitimate ground of action; and until the sinner is capable of a higher motive, he can act from no other. He was moved by the fear of evil, of loss, of ruin, and of punishment.[13] But after adoption into God's family, the soul is not only capable of higher motives, it is required to act from them—the highest of which is love: the love for God, for holiness, the kingdom of righteousness, and for all mankind.

As McCabe also pointed out, one must seek holiness with "primary reference" to rectitude, justice and holiness:

a "love of moral purity, a longing for holiness, a desire to be created anew in Christ Jesus."

Different Conditions

The conditions to be met also mark the difference between the two groups of seekers. That is, the requirements of the two groups differ. One has to repent, confess, forsake his sin and believe in order to be pardoned. The other has to make an entire consecration, believe and obey God to have his nature cleansed. In each case, the will cooperates to its fullest possible limits, but the renewed and regenerated will has more to do and is able to do more than before. In seeking pardon, the will decided "to forego sinful indulgences." "In full redemption, the will is required to surrender itself." And as McCabe suggests: "it is easier to give up an act than it is to surrender the will itself and bind it to conform to and acquiesce in the will of another forever."

Another vital element in this connection is mentioned by McCabe: "Suppose God should cleanse a soul from all alienation to Himself, and from all inbred depravity, without its own deliberate and undivided choice of holiness—without its exercising the faith that defnitely claims the great blessing—and without being actuated by those high and holy motives which center in God—such an act would be a marked departure from that principle of His economy so uniformly observed, namely never to do for an accountable being that which he can do for himself."[14] That would deprive the soul of the free exercise of its own power of choice, and would prevent its achieving the excellence and development of character that comes from voluntarily choosing the higher state when to remain in the lower is possible. It requires decision (will), effort and faith to rise above the common plane of life.

Entire Sanctification: A Covenant Work

Any experience of grace in the soul is received in consequence of (1) Its free choice of the experience; and (2) Its specific faith, or faith with specific reference to the thing sought. Therefore, it may be asked: "Why should pardon be presented to the soul for acceptance or rejection, and sanctification be wrought in the soul without its enjoying the exalted privilege of accepting that gift, and of relying specifically upon the blood of atonement for it?" Salvation is a covenant work and requires man's cooperation: (1) His will to be saved; and (2) His faith to be saved. This is also required for man's cleansing from all sin.

Man will not seek cleansing until he is convinced of the awfulness of sin in God's sight, and that an infected soul is the breeding ground for acts of sin. He must see his own sinful state and realize how such a state grieves God who is holy, who created man holy, who wants man to be holy, and who provides for man's holiness. One of the great proofs of man's depravity and need of cleansing is not his great outward acts of sin but his complacency in a state of sinfulness; and his willingness to be less than he could be for God, who has redeemed him at such cost.

This Is A Subsequent Crisis

The faithfulness of God to fulfill His promise to cleanse the soul subsequent to its being forgiven of its actual transgressions is seen in the cases of the Apostles who were converted and then cleansed; of the Samaritans who had two crisis experiences; in the case of Cornelius (although that has been disputed by many); in the case of the Ephesians, the Thessalonians, the Romans, and the Corinthians. A careful study of the Word of God will reveal that the Birth of the Spirit must precede the Baptism with the Spirit, forgiveness must precede cleansing; and the first crisis of the grace of God in the soul is with the second crisis of cleansing in view.

In taking this position, we are in agreement with modern psychiatry which has discovered the therapeutic value of a trauma—or shock—which is used increasingly to restore one to normalcy.

We do not deny the fact and value of a "process"—or development—but we believe that every process has its crisis which is closely related to what preceded and followed it. In the matter of the soul's second crisis, it refers to moral fitness rather than any fact of finality, or achievement beyond which there is no progress.

Sin is "a psychological unity" (White) which cannot be

removed in parts. It stays or goes as a unit. Any remaining trace of sin has in it the elements and possibilities of all sin. That is why any remaining cancer cell causes concern to the doctors. There is no such thing as the division of the evil principle or carnal mind and of its removal a part at a time, or piecemeal.

Sin and sins are related as cause and effect. Our question concerns deliverance from sin—perfect soul health. Therefore, we must recognize the twofold nature of sin: (1) as an act which produces guilt, that requires forgiveness or pardon; (2) as a polluted state or a diseased nature which requires cleansing or healing. Back of these sinful acts which become visible in the outward conduct, there lies a polluted nature of which the unsanctified is painfully conscious.

Man's "double need" demands a "double cure." "Sin commited, and depravity felt, are very different: the one is an action, the other a state of the affections. The regenerate believer is saved from the one, and he has grace to enable him to have victory over the other; but the disposition itself to some extent remains, under the control of a stronger power implanted, but still making resistance, and indicating actual presence, and needing to be entirely sanctified."[15]

While this experience of holiness is "a crisis"—an act, something done in a moment, instantaneously—it is "a crisis with a view to a process" as Principal Moule of Cambridge expressed it. It is "God's original cure for original sin" and while "the Bible tells us what God does with inbred sin . . . it does not fully inform us as to how He does it." But our lack of knowledge on the "modus operandi" is no excuse for a neutral position on the fact of full deliverance from all sin.

"Protestant theology is doomed unless it can discover or recover a doctrine of entire sanctification. . . . The best philosophical thought of our day points to the possibility and necessity of such an experience. . . . The theology of a message of entire sanctification is valid."[16]

This Crisis Experience Is Possible

To teach that one cannot live without sin is to teach that a just God has made a law one cannot obey. Since God never demands the impossible, the unnecessary, or the unreasonable of any one, we believe and teach that this experience can be realized in this life.

Dr. Henry C. Sheldon presents the possibility of this present personal experience in these words:

"Can a man advance here to a state which may be described negatively as free from sin, and positively as under the complete dominion of love—a state in which the moral disposition is pure and normal through and through, and conduct fails to be ideal in all respects only through unavoidable creaturely limitations? It must be granted that observation teaches us that the period of earthly discipline is in general all too short to consummate in this sense the work of sanctification. But, on the other hand, where is the warrant for assuming that such a consummation is strictly impossible? Philosophy certainly does not afford it, that is, a philosophy that is consonant with Christian principles. It cannot be said that the body is an insuperable obstacle to entire sanctification, for Christian truth does not allow that there is any essential evil in matter. If there is, then, any insuperable obstacle, it must be in the spirit. The human spirit is indeed finite, fallible, and infirm; but not one of these qualities stands in necessary opposition to holiness. As for the sinful bias with which it is affected, who can say on grounds of reason that it is beyond remedy within the limits of earthly life? Great moral transformations are wrought in very brief intervals of time. Who then is authorized to affirm that it is beyond the competency of God's remedial agency to completely sanctify a soul before death?

"A rational warrant for denying the possibility of entire sanctification in this life being thus wanting, the ground of denial must be found, if discovered at all, in revelation. It must be proved that the Scriptures teach that it is outside of the divine ability or the divine purpose to consummate the sanctification of any subject of grace before the article of death. Calvinists are hindered, of course, by their postulates from assuming that it is beyond the divine ability to do this; and non-Calvinists must needs despair of sustaining this assumption from the Scriptures, in the face of such words as those of Paul, which describe

God as 'able to do exceeding abundantly above all that we ask or think.' It remains then to deduce from the Scriptures that it is outside of the divine purpose, or no part of the divine economy, to bring any one to the point of entire sanctification in this life. But who has ever made a deduction of this sort which has even the appearance of legitimacy?"[17]

Mr. Wesley's views on this point need frequent emphasis. In brief, they are:
    (1) There is such a thing as Christian Perfection.
    (2) It is that love of God and our neighbor, which implies deliverance from all sin.
    (3) It is received merely by faith.
    (4) It is not so early as justification.
    (5) It is not so late as death.
    (6) It is given instantaneously, in one moment.
    (7) It is to be expected now, every moment.
    (8) It is improvable.
    (9) It is amissable, capable of being lost.
    (10) It is constantly both preceded and followed by a gradual work.
    (11) None can deny that an instantaneous change has been wrought in some believers.[18]

Dr. McCabe quotes Mr. Wesley as saying: "I believe justification to be wholly distinct from sanctification, and necessarily antecedent to it. . . .'. All who enjoy sanctification assert that they sought it as a distinct blessing."[19]

The Calvinistic view, in brief, is that during man's life "there abide still some remnants of corruption in every part of his nature; and that every man 'doth daily break' God's law in thought, word, and deed."

The decline of positive Methodist theology paved the way for a revival of Calvinism. But despite man's declarations to the contrary, God has provided this experience for man in this present life (Luke 1:74, 75). We teach that man may live without sinning, but can sin. Others teach that man cannot live without sinning.

This Crisis Experience is Purposeful

Man's need of salvation is vividly expressed by Dr. Harold Paul Sloan whom we quote by his personal permission. He described "the tragic predicament of the natural man" in these words:

"Clearly there is something abnormal about the natural man. His inner life has somehow got out of balance . . . and as a consequence (he) finds himself continually driven by an unbalanced awareness of 'I' that develops four great falsehoods—

> "(1) The lust of self-sufficiency (joy in the independent adequacy of self);
>
> "(2) The lust of self-assertion (joy in the assertive expression of self);
>
> "(3) The lust of pride (joy in a completely irrational glorification of self);
>
> "(4) The lust for possession (which is partly an expression of pride and partly of desire for security . . .)

"Self-driven man feels the call of the infinite, the sublime, the eternal; but he is shut away from them by the narrowness of his self-centered outlook. He is too large for time, but too small for eternity. To live as a dying animal, he is very much too large. To live as a son of God, he is very much too small. He is a creature greatly out of balance and needing salvation."[20]

And this moral tragedy is "not a tragedy which God wills upon him. It is rather a tragedy he created for himself by his false use of his freedom."[21]

There are some basic, divinely-revealed truths connected with this subject of true holiness—or full salvation: (1) Christ's death provides salvation for all men everywhere who will to be saved; (2) Christ's salvation provides for all of man's spiritual needs; (3) Christ's salvation relates to the present life as well as to the future life.

In order to escape the personal responsibility for facing these problems, man tries to interpret these truths in such a manner as to appease his mind and heart. (1) One of the ways by which man seeks to shun his personal responsibility is to take refuge behind the decrees of God and a limited atonement. (2) Another way is to describe man's nature as being such that so long as he is in the body full deliverance from sin is impossible. That admits that partial salvation is the most any one can expect in this life. (3)

Others have developed a teaching of imputation which represents man as being considered holy, when in reality he is not holy. (4) Others have so departmentalized salvation into sections or works of grace associated with crises, that each one of its several parts seems isolated rather than vitally associated.

In reality, there is but one salvation and all its phases are vitally related:

Justification (initial salvation) is in order to

Sanctification (full salvation), which is in order to

Glorification (final salvation). These constitute one perfect whole to which each sustains a vital relation.

Mr. Wesley says: "By salvation I mean, not barely, according to the vulgar notion, deliverance from hell, or going to heaven; but a present deliverance from sin, a restoration of the soul to its primitive health, its original purity; a recovery of the divine nature; the renewal of our souls after the image of God, in righteousness and true holiness, in justice, mercy and truth. This implies all holy and heavenly tempers, and, by consequence, all holiness of conversation.

"Now, if by salvation we mean a present salvation from sin, we cannot say holiness is the condition of it, for it is the thing itself. Salvation in this sense, and holiness, are synonymous terms. . . ."[22]

"All The Motives Are Love"

Dr. Harold Paul Sloan speaks of the "sanctified experience" as one's finding "every choice of life rising out of a fellowship-consciousness, rich at once with a sense of guidance, and with a motive of grateful love. . . . Christian perfection is thus a true perfection in this sense only that all the believer's motives are now love. Every choice is motivated by a warm, enriching sense of presence and fellowship. Christ and he live one life together, and the motive of the life is always 'the love of Christ constraineth me.' "[23]

Bishop Foster in his *Merrick Lectures,* asked: "What is this higher grace? Some call it holiness; some sanctification; some perfection; some maturity. There has been much unseemly disputation over the name as well as much fanatical profession concerning the experience, and much crude and unsound teaching as to what it includes and how it is to be obtained, and much ill-tempered criticism.

"It answers all the ends of description to say that it is the perfecting of the soul in love. Love is not simply the queen of the graces, but the mother of them all—the all-embracing. Love is the fulfilling of the law, love made perfect excludes envy, jealousy, pride, and all violent and hurtful tempers and acts. . . . Perfection of holy love is the perfection of saintship. The cultivation of every other grace is prompted by love, and all growth in them is measured by and is heightened by love. . . . While it reigns, there is no place for evil thoughts, evil desires, evil feelings. Heaven has already come. Can it be permanent at its highest pitch? . . . Not as an emotion. . . . But as a principle governing the life, we are bold to say love may and should abide moment by moment and without alloy."[24]

Experientially it is being cleansed from sin (I John 1:7), being made free from sin (Romans 6:18); the putting to death of the old man (Romans 6:6) by which he is destroyed (I John 3:8); the heart is made perfect in love (I John 4:17); it is to be pure in heart (Matt. 5:8); without spot (Eph. 5:27), and holy (I Peter 1:15); and it solves in one's experience "the language of I Thess. 5:23." It is the "inward cleansing underlying external rectitude."

This purity is required: Matt. 5:8; I Tim. 1:5; 5:22. It is provided: Titus 2:14; Heb. 9:13, 14; I John 1:7; 3:3. It is experienced: Acts 15:8, 9; I Peter 1:22; Psalms 24:4.

The supreme purpose is to make us like Christ in character and conduct. It is to enable the believer to do the will of God patiently, effectively, with naturalness and ease, or to suffer the will of God with patience and good cheer. It is also intimately associated with power for service (Luke 24:49; Acts 1:8).

A writer who does not espouse the Wesleyan-Arminian interpretation of holiness declared the purpose of the Spirit's fullness to be:

"(1) The realization of Christ's abiding presence.
"(2) The reproduction of Christ's holy life in the believer.
"(3) The re-enactment of Christ's supernatural power through us."[25]

This experience has two aspects: *Subjective,* or its effect upon or within us—one's personal response to God's call and claim; and *objective,* or its relation to God's will for man—or the aim He has in view—it is what God claims for His use or as His possession. And one has well said that the answer to Christ's prayer in John 17:17 is "the subjective realization of objective holiness." We believe that God intends that these two phases, which are distinct in thought, should not be separated in actual personal experience.

This Crisis Experience Is Conditional

Just as there are conditions for justification, or initial salvation, so there are conditions for full salvation or entire sanctification. They are man's part of the covenant. Salvation is a covenant work involving two parties: God and man.

1. There must be a genuine conversion from the old life, for birth must precede baptism.
2. There must be a positive conviction of one's soul need, which produces definite, determined seeking.
3. There must be a complete separation from sin. We cannot be cleansed while we consciously cling to sin, or to the love of the world which destroys the love of God.
4. There must be an entire consecration to the whole will of God. This involves, as Oswald Chambers has reminded us, "self-renunciation," "self-denial," and "self-crucifixion," as well as the courage to suffer the consequences thereof.
5. There also must be the claiming of one's inheritance. Here is where personal appropriating faith enters. But one must be certain that he has met the antecedent conditions if faith is to become operative. It is a crude illustration, but to me faith is like one of these automatic elevators: when all conditions are met, it works. But if everything about it is not properly coordinated, you get no response. You may tease and hope, fret and fume—but you get nowhere. But let one appear who knows how

to meet the conditions for operating it, and behold, it works!

This Crisis Experience Is Perilous

Like every other spiritual truth, it may be abused. Its enemies scorn it, and its friends often misrepresent it and fail to maintain it in the true perspective. Misplaced emphases often distort this precious truth and make it a caricature instead of the masterpiece God intended it to be. But abuse by some is no excuse for others' neglect or rejection. Faith has been abused and reduced to mere mental assent. Good works have degenerated into a "bookkeeping religion." The keeping power of Christ has been abused by unconditional eternal security.

Some deny any need for it, claiming they were cleansed at conversion. Others say it is impossible of realization; therefore, to seek it is vanity. Some claim that one has to be holy before he can consecrate himself to God. Others claim that one may be consecrated, yet remain unholy. And many who had obtained a clean heart lost it by not maintaining the condition wherein purity was possible. The late Rev. Joseph H. Smith declared: "No one has ever yet reached any height in the grace of God but that some one who had been there before him fell to his doom from that lofty height. Let us take heed lest we fall."

Any underestimating the crisis aspect of the experience tends to put one on the road toward naturalism—or self-sanctification. And by settling down in an unfavorable environment one fails to reach his goal. He excludes the supernatural and is caught in the maelstrom of moral relaxation and soon is victimized by the devil. Modernism says: "Relax." God says: "Repent." Modernism encourages "lysis" instead of "crisis," or salvation by culture instead of by the grace of God. Our need is for more radical crisis experiences of moral transformations.

Modern religious leaders are afraid of the emotional reactions if they cultivate deep spirituality. We are suffering from an intellectual recoil against emotional expression and are dying for the lack of definite crisis experiences in the lives of professing Christians.

Our churches should pray as Samuel Chadwick's

church prayed: for God to raise a Lazarus from their midst. He sent them a poor drunkard. His was a crisis experience—with glorious consequences. Beware of that spirit which by opposing this crisis experience of cleansing (1) Denies the Word of God, (2) Disputes Reason, (3) and Disregards Credible Human Testimony which is corroborated by holy living.

The greatest peril in connection with this crisis of cleansing is that many believers consider it too idealistic and too theoretical; hence, do not press on to obtain it. "The New Testament gives no ground for supposing that there is such an absolute contrast between the conditions of the heavenly life and those of Christian life in this world that sin must be entirely alien to the one and inevitable in the other. In the absence of such a contrast, the commands, instructions, and prayers which look to entire sanctification or perfect love, carry a certain presumption that the state which these terms define is of possible attainment in this life. It must be confessed, however, that it stands forth as an exceedingly high ideal. Anyone who understands all that it implies will despair of its possibility, save as his heart is quickened by a large and intense faith in the marvelous power of divine grace."[26]

If tempted to consider its demands too rigid, then think of the self-denying Son of God who suffered to make it possible.

If you fear it unnecessary, remember God's justice: He never requires the unnecessary, impossible, or unreasonable.

If you consider the standard too high, remember that Jesus exemplified its spirit in every detail of His life.

If you are perplexed as to the way into this glorious experience, follow Him who is "The Way, The Truth, and The Life."

If you consider your case a difficult one, bear in mind that nothing is "too hard for the Lord."

If you think that your need is not as great as others: "All have sinned . . ." and God is "no respecter of persons."

If you are deterred for any reason—observe Him as He prays for you to have this inheritance, stand near His cross as He dies to procure it for you, ponder His exceeding great and precious promises to you; appreciate your privileges as a child of God who is being fitted here for eternal residence and fellowship with the Christ whose glory you shall behold throughout eternity—and then press your claim for your inheritance among them that are sanctified by faith. Then, and only then, will your life be "a constant pageant of triumph," through Him who is able to deliver from the guilt of sin, from the power of sin, and from the love of sin—as well as to fully save the trusting soul from the inbeing of sin; and who doth so deliver all who come unto Him for this crisis of cleansing.

CHAPTER FIVE

True Holiness: Its Progressive Aspects
I Peter 1:2
II Peter 1:1-8

In our last study, we considered the crisis aspect of the experience of true holiness. In this one, we shall devote ourselves to a study of this experience as a "continuation" after the crisis: the progressive development of that obtained in the crisis. It is not only important to know what we seek, and how to obtain it; but to know that we have obtained it. We must know how to keep what we have obtained; how to cultivate our inheritance, how to invest and enlarge our spiritual birthright, how to go on from spiritual purity toward spiritual maturity.

Perhaps one of the causes for much of the spiritual mortality rate among professors of this high experience is because of the great mistake in supposing that "the gracious life once implanted in the believer's heart will be retained without effort." There may—and will—be "changes of emotion . . . without radical changes of character" (Bishop Foster); but many are seduced into things which cause them to forfeit their acceptance with God. We are greatly concerned to discover what the entirely sanctified may do not only to retain the results of that gracious crisis but to develop it to its fullest possible extent.

Doubtless some of the apparent indifference to the aspect of continuance beyond the crisis has been produced by an imbalance in the emphases by two extremely different groups. (1) One group declares that the crisis is all-important. They are so anxious to maintain that aspect they seem to overlook its subsequent involvements. (2) The other group denies the need for a crisis, and declares that one grows into holiness. They stress repression and cultivation. We need to avoid both extremes. Each substitutes one phase of the truth for the whole truth.

Much of the confusion on these points could be avoided by discriminating carefully between "grace and growth." The Rev. Isaiah Reid sets the difference forth thus:

"Grace is of God; growth is of man.

"Grace is conferred; growth is commanded.

"Grace is a favor; growth is a duty.

"Grace is administered; growth is attained.

"Grace is before growth; for a thing that is not cannot grow.

"Grace is the unmerited helpfulness of God administered in love.

"Growth is the enlarging of the ways of God's helpfulness within us, and the exercise of what is given in such ways that there is continued increase.

"Growth is but the cooperation of the human spirit, and belongs to the man side of the question of salvation. Growth does not create or begin any grace, or gift, or faculty. It has reference always to the exercise of any of these unto more godliness. Growth is never into, but always in, grace.

"Grace is like the air we breathe, or the water for which we thirst—all good of themselves, all free; but all of no avail unless appropriated and individually used.

"Grace refers first to this personal appropriation, and next to the enlargement that comes from so doing."[1]

The Purpose: Growth in Holiness

The words Peter uses are significant. In I Peter 1:2 and II Peter 2:1, we find "multiply" used; and in II Peter 1:5, the word used is "add"—or properly translated, "furnish"—as one would "furnish a house already built with additional comforts, or better equipment for greater usefulness and effectiveness."

Thus as we face this question of continuation, the purposes are: (1) To multiply the grace given unto us, (2) To enlarge the faculties we possess, (3) To increase our skill in the use of our powers and faculties, (4) To develop greater wisdom in our application to duty, (5) To increase our capacity for enlarged and more effective service—to the end that we may become more like Christ in inward character and dispositions, as well as outward conduct, that God might be glorified.

"In the happy experience of a full redemption from sin, and with the Holy Ghost's power upon us and in us, do not let us conclude that we have reached the climax of Christian character; that there is no need of growth in grace we have thus gloriously received from God. In fact, that is but the beginning of true spiritual progress. We are not finished, packed, and labeled for glory, with nothing to do but rejoice in our glorious experience. We are to develop and upon a symmetrical pattern. Not simply one virtue, or some faculties of our spiritual manhood, but the whole man, upon the pattern of Christ Jesus. The seven distinct colors of the spectrum are necessary to form a true beam of light; so the Christian character is to be complete and harmonious in all the elements which compose it.

"One man's piety has too much fiery 'red,' or passionate zeal; another, the cadaverous 'blue,' a long-faced sanctimony; another, the uncertain 'green,' as of immaturity; another, the sallow 'yellow' of feeble decrepitude; and another the sweet 'violet' of a sickly sentimentality. The growth or development must be harmonious and symmetrical; and, because a man has one strong point in his character, do not let him therefore conclude that he is perfect and rounded, and has no further need of growth, so as to be the beautiful composite of the Christly spirit and character."[2]

This Continuation Is Vital to Personal Experience

Entire sanctification prepares the way for it "by removing the chief inward hindrances": (1) mixed motives and (2) double-mindedness. This is growth in measure, not in kind. Our "powers are improvable and our capacities are expansive" (Reid). The fact that very few people seem to appreciate their possibilities should rebuke those who believe that the crisis is the goal!

Perfection is not finality, any more than health hinders growth. "One perfected in love may grow far swifter than he did before" (Wesley). Bishop J. Paul Taylor says: "Pentecost is not a finality. It does not set us on a summit of ultimate spiritual privilege. It is the perfect preparation for the real exploration of our inheritance in Christ."[3]

"Sanctification brings the intellect of the Christian into captivity to Christ, so that he thinks for Him; puts the love of God in his heart; so that he is unselfish and beneficient; the life of righteousness into his conscience, so that the law of right is his rule; the life of obedience into his will, so that it is his meat and drink to do the will of the Father."[4]

The individual has an obligation to continue the development of his personal experience. To fail to do so results in arrested development of the spiritual life—producing spiritual dwarfs. To fail to grow produces shallowness in spiritual perception and superficial professors of true holiness. The possibility of almost unlimited development carries with it the personal responsibility to accept one's duty. It will require intense effort but we must concentrate on it. One may shirk his responsibility, but he cannot shift it. "To place all the responsibility upon Christ is presumption; and to assume all responsibility without Him is conceit."[5]

The crisis places one on "the threshold of all blessedness," but the development requires continuing and consistent effort. A tremendous responsibility rests on those who have experienced the crisis of cleansing. "They are to develop their characters . . . master their infirmities . . . break out of their limitations and disadvantages wherever possible . . . practice self-denial . . . arm themselves with a mind to suffer. . . . They must suffer poverty that some other may be rich . . . know how to be abased and how to abound . . . love some things and hate some things . . . live yet reckon themselves to be dead . . . be pilgrims and strangers, and kings and priests . . . that He may be glorified in them and they in Him."[6]

The crisis is a step, which lengthens into a life which is composed of a series of successive and correlated acts. But at each moment, there is absolute dependence upon Christ through personal appropriating faith, for heaven is not reached by one leap from the cross, "But by daily walking with God. . . . The promises and provisions of grace are so full that no honest soul need fear but that he will be kept safely by the power of God, through faith unto salvation."[7]

The divine requirements for us are: (1) "proportioned to the powers of each individual"; and (2) "a steady progress in love harmonizing with our circumstances and our increasing capacity and ability." Which means that "to love God . . . beyond our power or capacity—would be impossible; and to love Him less than the full measure of our power to love, would be short of His requirement."[8]

This continuation beyond the crisis is distinctly Wesleyan. Mr. Wesley did not believe in a "perfection of concluded development." He felt that "the Christian life is a development in love."[9] Mr. Wesley in Sermon XXXV says: "There is no perfection of degrees, as it is termed; none which does not admit of a continual increase. So that how much soever any man has attained, or in how a degree soever he is perfect, he hath still need to 'grow in grace' and daily to advance in the knowledge and love of God his Saviour."[10]

On *"perfection of degrees"* Sugden says: "This rather curious phrase seems to mean a perfection which has reached the highest point, and is therefore not capable of any higher steps or degrees. This is a most important qualification of Wesley's teaching. As he says in the *Brief Thoughts* (1767) 'I believe in a gradual work both preceding and following that instant'; i.e., the instant of entire sanctification."[11]

Mr. Wesley not only believed that continuation was natural, but that it was discernible. In a letter to John Fletcher, dated March 22, 1775, Wesley wrote: "It is certain that every babe in Christ has received the Holy Ghost, and the Spirit witnesses with his spirit that he is a child of God. But he has not obtained Christian perfection. Perhaps you have not considered St. John's threefold distinction of Christian believers: little children, young men, and fathers. All of these had received the Holy Ghost, but only the fathers were perfected in love."[12]

Mr. Wesley and Mr. Fletcher and their contemporaries did not stress the "state of holiness" lest they seem to encourage settling down immediately following the crisis experience. But they did emphasize what Thomas Cook has described as maintaining the "condition of purity." That is, "a moment-by-moment salvation consequent upon a moment-by-moment obedience and trust. 'The blood of Jesus Christ cleanseth us from all sin' all the time by cleansing us every now." That enables one to better understand Wesley and Fletcher's incessant quest for more holiness; i.e., more love, regardless of any prior developments in the soul's relationship to God.

One went to the late Rev. Joseph H. Smith in a dilemma about the crisis experiences of the groups in Acts 2 and 4, for they seemed to be the same people, and in each case, the record is that "they were all filled with the Holy Ghost." Their question was: "Had these people lost their previous (Day of Pentecost) fullness?" Smith's reply was: "No, beloved! They had grown!" That is, they had continued their development and the ever-present God met their "ever-present need" with His "ever-present provision." It is "a disastrous error" when Christians content themselves with the grace received and endeavor to bring back past experiences instead of following on to know and to advance in holiness.

Holiness Is To Be Developed

When the crisis of cleansing is experienced, the "future progress" of the soul "consists of an increase in two distinct kinds of holiness. The first is a communicated holiness and is the direct work of the Spirit. The second is a developed holiness and is the result of obedience, education, and following the example of Christ. Through all eternity, these two causes will jointly secure the progress of the soul in moral purity. . . ."[13]

"There is a sense in which perfecting holiness should characterize the sanctified believer, after the work of cleansing has been made complete; that is, in the development and maturity of all the Christian graces. Sanctification brings the soul into the best possible condition for growth of grace and for the development of the fruit of the Spirit. Growth should then be rapid. The soul's powers should expand, and the character and life should constantly exhibit an increasing conformity to the perfect model furnished by Jesus Christ.

"The sanctified soul should also be contantly perfecting the manifestation of holiness. Many things render the manifestation of holiness quite imperfect in those who are wholly sanctified. Difference in temperament will effect a difference in the manifestation of spiritual life in two individuals equally holy. William Cowper was naturally despondent and subject to attacks of melancholia. Some have charged it upon religion that he was so often and so greatly depressed. That is a sad mistake. Doubtless, his religion is all that kept him from desperation and self-destruction at times."[14]

This Continuation Is Admonished in the Bible

Regardless of the logic of any position, when it concerns his soul's eternal destiny, the glory of God, and the service of his fellowmen, man craves divine authority. Therefore, when he asks: "Where does the Bible support this view?" the answer is found in part in *I John 1:7*—"But if we walk in the light, as he is in the light, we have fellowship one with another and the blood of Jesus Christ his Son cleanseth us from all sin."

On this verse, Pardington wrote: "Here the Greek verb translated 'cleanseth' is in the present tense, indicative mood, and its force is to express continuous action in present time. Literally, as already mentioned, it may be rendered 'keeps cleansing,' or, even better, 'keeps on cleansing.' The idea is this: if we keep walking (here the verb is in the present subjunctive denoting continuous action, too) in the light, the blood will keep cleansing us: and the result will be that we shall have fellowship one with another. That is, primarily, the child of God will have fellowship with the Father; and, secondarily, the children of God will have fellowship with one another."[15]

Adam Clarke's comment on this passage is: "continues to cleanse us, i.e., to keep clean what it has made clean."

Man's Part of the Process

II Corinthians 7:1—"Having therefore these promises, dearly beloved, let us cleanse ourselves from all filthiness of the flesh and spirit, perfecting holiness in the fear of God."

It will be helpful to note what some standard commentators say on this verse. Let us first consider the Presbyterian, Albert Barnes:

"... Perfecting. This word means properly to bring an end, to finish, complete. The idea here is that of carrying it out to the completion. Holiness had been commenced in the heart, and the exhortation of the apostle is, that they should make every effort that it might be complete in all its parts.... It is an obligation which results from the nature of the law of God and His unchangeable claims on the soul. ... The obligation to be perfect is one that is unchangeable and eternal. . . . In the fear of God. Out of fear and reverence of God. From a regard to His commands, and a reverence for His name. The idea seems to be that we are always in the presence of God; and we should be awed and restrained by a sense of His presence from the commission of sin, and from indulgence in the pollutions of the flesh and spirit."[16]

Wesley's Notes: "Let us cleanse ourselves—This is the latter part of the exhortation, which was proposed, II Cor. 6:1, and resumed, verse 14. From all pollution of the flesh—All outward sin. And of the spirit—All inward. Yet, let us not rest in negative religion, but perfect holiness—Carrying it to the height in all its branches, and enduring to the end in the loving fear of God, the sure foundation of all holiness."[17]

II Peter 3:18—"But grow in grace, and in the knowledge of our Lord and Saviour Jesus Christ. To him be glory both now and forever, Amen." On this, Adam Clarke, the Methodist Commentator and Theologian says: "But grow in grace. Increase in the image and favor of God; every grace and Divine influence which ye have received is a seed, a heavenly seed, which, if it be watered with the dew of heaven from above, will endlessly increase and multiply itself. He who continues to believe, love, and obey, will grow in grace, and continually increase in the knowledge of Jesus Christ, as his sacrifice, sanctifier, counsellor, preserver, and final Saviour. The life of a Christian is a growth; he is at first born of God, and is a little child; becomes a young man, and a father in Christ. Every father was once an infant; and had he not grown, he would have never been a man. Those who content themselves with the grace they received when converted to God, are, at best, in a continual state of infancy; but we find, in the order of nature, that the infant that does not grow, and grow daily, too, is sickly and soon dies; so, in the order of grace, those who do not grow up into Jesus Christ are sickly, and will soon die, die to all sense and influence of heavenly things.

"There are many who boast of the grace of their conversion; persons who were never more than babes, and have long since lost even that grace, because they did not grow in it. Let him that readeth understand."[18]

Mr. Wesley says: "But grow in grace—That is, in every Christian temper. There may be, for a time, grace without growth; as there may be natural life without growth. But such sickly life, of soul or body, will end in death, and every day draw nigher to it. Health is the means of both natural and spiritual growth. . . . The end and design of grace being purchased and bestowed on us, is to destroy the image of the earthly, and restore us to that of the heavenly. And so far as it does this, it truly profits us; and also makes way for more of the heavenly gift, that we may at last be filled with all the fullness of God. The strength and wellbeing of a Christian depend on what his soul feeds on, as the health of the body depends on whatever we make our daily food. If we feed on what is according to our nature, we grow; if not, we pine away and die. The soul is of the nature of God, and nothing but what is according to His holiness can agree with it. Sin, of every kind, starves the soul, and makes it consume away. Let us not try to invert the order of God in His new creation: we shall only deceive ourselves. It is easy to forsake the will of God, and follow our own: but this will bring leanness into the soul. It is easy to satisfy ourselves without being possessed of the holiness and happiness of the gospel."[19]

Albert Barnes' observation is very illuminating: "No one becomes eminently pious, any more than one becomes eminently learned or rich, who does not intend to; and ordinarily, men, in religion, are what they design to be. They have about as much religion as they wish, and possess about the character which they intend to possess. When men reach extraordinary elevations in religion like

Baxter, Payson, and Edwards, they have gained only what they meant to gain; and the gay and worldly professors of religion, who have little comfort and peace, have in fact the character which they designed to have. If these things are so, then we may see the priority of the injunction to 'grow in grace'; and then, too, we may see the reason why so feeble attainments are made in piety by the great mass of those who profess religion."[20]

Something Beyond the Foundation

Hebrews 6:1—"Therefore, leaving the principles of the doctrine of Christ, let us go on unto perfection; not laying again the foundation of repentance from dead works, and of faith toward God."

On this, the Cambridge Greek New Testament says that the intent of the exhortation is not the overthrow, the neglect, or the forgetting of the things mentioned. Instead, they ought to be so familiar with them that they were able to "advance to less obvious knowledge"—go on to higher lessons that grew out of these foundational truths. "He invites his readers to advance with him to doctrines which lie beyond the range of rudimentary Christian teaching. . . . The 'perfection' intended is the full growth of those who are mature in Christian knowledge (see verse 14). . . . They ought not to be lingering among the elementary subjects of catechetical instruction. . . ."

Scott Family Bible suggests that what they were to "leave" were "not the most fundamental truths, or parts of Christianity; but the introductory elements, the lower and easier beginnings of it, as letters are the first principles or elements of learning. . . ." "Advance to a higher state of knowledge and holiness. . . . He would not linger around these elements in the discussion nor would he have them linger at the threshold of the Christian doctrines. . . ."[21]

We must remember that there is no standing still in religion. "It is impossible to maintain a halt in the Christian life; to stand still is to fall away. . . . This perfection is twofold: (1) maturity in religious knowledge, as a means; (2) full development of spiritual life as the end. It is sinful to remain only a babe in Christ and to have no wish to grow."[22]

"God is ever ready by the power of His Spirit to carry us forward to every degree of light, life, and love, necessary to prepare us for an eternal weight of glory. There can be little difficulty in attaining the end of our faith, the salvation of our souls from all sin, if God carry us forward to it; and this He will do if we submit to be saved in His own way and on His own terms. Many make a violent outcry against the doctrine of perfection, i.e., against the heart being cleansed from all sin in this life, and filled with love to God and man, because they judge it to be impossible! Is it too much to say of these that they know neither the Scripture nor the power of God? Surely the Scripture promises the thing; and the power of God can carry us on to the possession of it."[23]

One of the great scholars of the Holiness Movement, Dr. Daniel Steele, says: "This is the only other passage where this Greek word for perfection is found. It is here represented not as something realized by the lapse of time, or by unconscious growth, and, least of all, attainable only at death. We are exhorted to press on against wind and tide, till we reach this 'land of corn and wine and oil,' and take up our abode. For the Greek preposition 'unto' here embraces both motion to a place and rest in it, and cannot mean an aim at an unattainable ideal. . . . Here perfection 'refers especially to the fulness of spiritual knowledge manifesting itself in a Christian profession as the antithesis of babyhood,' spoken of in Heb. 5:13, 'Every one that partaketh of milk is without experience of the word of righteousness; for he is a babe.' This can be no other than the profession of Christian manhood, 'a perfect man unto the measure of the stature of the fulness of Christ'; i.e., in which one receives the fulness of Christ, the completeness of what He has to impart, a state of grace in which Paul not only was, but one in which he confidently expected to continue. 'And I know that when I come unto you, I shall come in the fullness of the blessing of Christ.' Rom. 15:29, R.V. Says Dr. Whedon, 'When Heb. vi. 1 is adduced as an exhortation to advancing to a perfected Christian character, it is no misquotation. It is the noun form of the Greek adjective rendered full age in the chapter v. 14, and signifies adulthood.' "[24]

Something Beyond Heart Purity

There is much food for serious thought in the words of William Jones, a brilliant minister of religion and an able doctor of medicine, who wrote: "Perfect love is equivalent to entire sanctification, but Christian perfection, in its legitimate sense, implies more than perfect love. The apostle uses the term 'perfection' in the sixth chapter of Hebrews as indicating a religious state in advance of the purification of the heart. He speaks of leaving the primary stages of Christian life and 'going on to perfection.' Heart purity is not the most advanced state of Christian life that is possible, and we assume that, according to the Divine plan, holiness is embraced in the primary stages of religious experience.

"The apostle states the case so clearly that no one can fail to apprehend the fact that there is very much of religious possibility lying beyond the period of sanctification, but that does not imply that the purification of the heart is a tedious or a protracted process. The entire Christian life is one of advancement. Progress is the law of the Divine procedure. The highest and broadest experience of a holy life is not attainable at once. . . .

"Conversion is an instantaneous work; so also sanctification, being a part of man's salvation is done at once. But Christian life has unlimited possibilities for development; it is continuous and progressive, but it is inseparable from correct doctrinal principles and right thinking; there is room for almost unlimited culture in holy living.

"The gospel proposes to make men perfect in the practice of Christian ethics, but it also proposed to make him skillful in the use of his intellectual faculties as a holy person.. . .

"Christian perfection is not an accidental appendage of the gospel system; its attainment is a duty obligatory upon all men. We are commanded to 'be perfect even as our Father in heaven is perfect.' This perfection implies more than the sanctification of the soul; it is a state where the graces are developed and the faculties trained in holy warfare. The Christian is exhorted to 'go on' to this perfection, and as life always precedes motion, we conclude no one is born in this state of perfection, and as the word here translated "perfect" is not synonymous with the term rendered purification, we are persuaded that it embraces more than purity. The word translated perfection signifies the end of effort—'completeness'—it indicates the mature fruitage of a holy life. The apostle uses the term to express that spiritual condition where the whole redeemed man shall stand before the world in the dignity of his perfect manhood. But heart purity is one of the primary principles of the Christian system. It is the Divine order that it should follow conversion speedily. Holiness necessarily precedes maturity. The world is greatly mistaken at this point; no one can mature perfectly who is not perfectly purified in early life. And all who are sanctified near the hour of death enter heaven in a state of immaturity. Neither is maturity a produce of age alone; a thousand influences contribute to maturity after the soul has been thoroughly sanctified.

"God in His wisdom did not make our entrance into heaven to depend on our maturity, but on our holiness. Holiness is fitness for heaven; perfection is fitness for successful work here or for anything God has for us here or hereafter.

"God deals with men as accountable beings, and He demands of the holiness teachers and evangelists of the present age perfect loyalty to His cause; they cannot overlook the wants of the present time; they must conform to the ethics of Holiness."[25]

Paul's Profession of Perfection

"Not as though I had already attained, either were already perfect; but I follow after, if that I may apprehend that for which also I am apprehended of Christ Jesus.

"Brethren, I count not myself to have apprehended: but this one thing I do, forgetting those things which are behind, and reaching forth unto those things which are before,

"I press toward the mark for the prize of the high calling of God in Christ Jesus.

"Let us therefore, as many as be perfect, be thus minded: and if in any thing ye be otherwise minded, God shall reveal even this unto you" (*Philippians 3:12-15*).

This Scripture has been the battleground on which there have been many contests as to whether or not Paul professed or disclaimed perfection. The truth is, he did both. There is a perfection which he professed and there is a perfection which he disclaimed; and a failure to distinguish between these two not only produces confusion, but involves one in error.

The perfection he disclaims (v. 12), is that final perfection or final salvation which the soul reaches when it passes out of the realm of probation when at death it "passes out of the sphere of possible sin." Whedon says that this is a higher perfection "which is different from but does not contradict the lower ... of verse 15, which belongs to the earthly Christian life, and to which St. Paul had attained."

"The mark—The goal, which is neither more nor less than absolute conformity to Christ. ... As many as be perfect—including himself in the class thus designated, and leaving each member of the Philippian Church to decide whether or not he himself belonged to it. (See note on verse 12.) The perfection here is a moral perfection, and, therefore, a different thing from that in verse 12 which the apostle declares himself not to have attained. ..."[26]

Dr. Harry Ironside says: "The apostle, therefore, is careful to make it clear that he did not claim to have reached a state of resurrection-perfectness while here upon earth. He uses a word, in this instance, which means completeness, that to which nothing can be added. This state, he declares, he had not already attained. But he had it in view, for he knew that, at the coming of the Lord Jesus Christ, he would be made like Himself, and thus free from all tendency to sin. ... The perfection of verse 15 is that of full growth. ..."[27]

While one may not approve of much that Ironside taught concerning holiness, he can approve his differentiating "resurrection-perfectness ... to which nothing can be added" which is for the future life, from the perfect deliverance from sin which we teach as possible in this present life. What we need to remember is that as long as man is in the body, he possesses "a possibility of sinning for such a possibility is indispensable to accountability. There also exists a susceptibility of sin, for such is indispensable to a state of probation. But these do not constitute a sinful tendency. They are entirely compatible with perfect holiness."[28]

Mr. Wesley declares that there is a difference between "one that is perfect, and one that is perfected. The one is fitted for the race, verse 15; the other, ready to receive the prize." What he pursues is "perfect holiness, preparatory to glory...." On verse 13, Mr. Wesley comments that Paul says he is "already possessed of perfect holiness," and of verse 14, he says: Paul is "pursuing with the whole bent and vigor of . . . soul, perfect holiness and eternal glory."

On this portion of Scripture, Maclaren suggests that the important thing in the soul's perfection is the ideal or direction of the moral character instead of the absolute attainment; for "men have in them the germ of a life which has no natural end but absolute completeness."

(Note: Those who are desirous of further help on these verses from Philippians 3 are referred to *The Adequate Man* by Dr. Paul S. Rees, pages 69-87.)

The Means of Grace Assist This Continuation

"There is set before us an eternal progression in holiness," but those who so live do not always manifest an exact equality in their graces. The elements of time cause a wide difference. So do the elements of capacity, temperament and circumstances. It is not essential to a holy life that it be without variations of experience and that there be even and equal emotions under all provocations; but there must be "unmoveable steadfastness of faith and the fullness of love"—for without these there is "no present attainment of full salvation; none, indeed in the present life...."[29]

The item of concern to us is how we may continue to grow in grace and accelerate the development of spiritual maturity.

The first thing is that we must avoid being satisfied with present attainments and "resting on the oars," drifting along with nothing to do but to enjoy ourselves. The end is the important thing. Our religion demands that we advance, but we need a robust religion that goes forth into the new and difficult, not because we see the end but because God has promised the end—and He is faithful (I Thess. 5:24).

The development of strength, the culture and polish and usefulness that come to the saved, are contingent upon their own efforts; those qualities are resultants; they are inseparable from time and are of necessity gradual and progressive. The universal law of growth is by appropriation and has reference to the development of proportions or the increase of strength.

There must be conscientious and faithful activity in spiritual things, subject to the Spirit's guidance. Love must be the actuating principle of this life and there must be a constant guard against sin. Eternal vigilance is the price of purity. And furthermore, any degree of temptation must be resisted.

The Holy Spirit, "the Educator of the soul" (Barry), knows His own ends and His own means; therefore, let us carefully follow all His leadings as He develops us in this life of maturing holiness. Of this we may be sure: our symmetrical development will require prayer, meditation, Bible study, Christian fellowship, and a proper observance of the Sacraments, as well as constant, comprehensive consecration.

There must be a steadfast faith, which is the "mysterious hand by which the holy soul clings to God amid all temptations, and is kept from sin" (Bishop Foster). It is through trusting God that we learn to live by the minute—undisturbed and undistracted, "Careful for nothing." (That is: "Anxious for nothing.") And in order to reach that place there must be deadness to the appeals and allure of the world that would in any wise interfere with the soul's devotion to God.

This Continuation Is With Eternity In View

"It is a universal belief among Christians that entire sanctification, and by implication perfection in love, are absolutely essential qualifications for entrance into the heavenly abode. . . . The one positive and exclusive teaching of the Scriptures with reference to the purifying of the spiritual nature is that the work is wrought by virtue of the atonement made by Christ and by the direct and immediate agency of the Holy Spirit (I Cor. 6:11). . . .

"It is to be feared that many who believe in the attainability of entire purity and unalloyed love do not seriously desire to enter into that state and live in accordance with its requirements, presuming that God will accomplish at the time of their death what they practically refuse to have Him do for them during their lives."[30]

The true end of all religion is the renewal of man in the image of God; and "the essence and prize of Methodism is sanctity, or the moral transformation of the heart and life of man."[31] "Salvation is seen as a process by which man passes through a series of successive stages, each state representing a different and higher level."[32] Thus we are reminded anew that salvation is used in a wide sense: Sometimes it includes present and final salvation—"salvation in its inception, continuation, and conclusion." Sometimes it refers only to present salvation as embracing justification and sanctification, with the emphasis laid on sanctification. Mr. Wesley said: "By salvation, I mean not barely, according to the vulgar notion, deliverance from hell, or going to heaven; but a present deliverance from sin, a restoration of the soul to its primitive health, its original purity; a recovery of the divine nature; the renewal of our souls after the image of God, in righteousness and true holiness, in justice, mercy, and truth. This implies all holy and heavenly tempers and, by consequence, all holiness of conversation."[33]

"The goal of the whole process of salvation is the entire sanctification of man. This is the condition of final justification, or final salvation and glorification beyond the grave."[34]

Mr. Wesley blended, with Scripture warrant, the idea of the gradual development with an instantaneous element, as the divinely-revealed process of salvation. By this means, he gave the order of salvation "the form of a process aiming at the perfection of man." But by perfection, he meant more than what is sometimes called "full sanctification."

"In the order of salvation, sanctification has its place between justification and final salvation." Sanctification involves a real change in man. "It is only through sanctification that man becomes qualified for final salvation and glorification.... Incorporated in a process of salvation aiming at the sanctity which is a necessary qualification for eternal life, it is clear that sanctification must become the dominant component in salvation."[35]

Something For Us To Do

The admonition "Let us go on" serves a twofold purpose. One is *Preventive*: One can't go back if he goes forward; and to go forward, one must leave some things and go in for other and greater things. The other purpose is *Preparative*: Our usefulness depends upon our development. One needs not only character, but experience and skill. By going on, after leaving, one is prepared or fitted for even greater service and honor. The depth of our interest will be proved by our "energy of pursuit." Whatever this costs us, it is wonderful to realize that God's design is to fit us for eternal communion with Him and all the redeemed in the glory.

"Paint and picture the glories of the world beyond the confines of time and sense as wonderful as the most vivid imagination is capable, and we may still be absolutely sure that the reality far exceeds anything which the human mind has ever conceived. We can be perfected in love in this life. The little child can love God with all the powers of its limited mind, might, and strength; and so the aged saint, with many years of experience and of intellectual and spiritual development, can perfectly love God in proportion to his capacity; but we may rest assured that the most advanced of all the saints that have ever walked this earth have at the close of life but just commenced their eternal career. Ever advancing, ever rising, ever growing, ever climbing loftier peaks of vision, they will go on from glory to glory while eternal ages shall roll their endless rounds. And this is partly because the environment or heaven is always and in all respects helpful. Blessed are the souls that shall overcome in all the conflicts of this earthly life by the blood of the Lamb and the word of their testimony....

"The possibilities of an eternal, blissful existence in the presence of our Lord and Saviour Jesus Christ, the companionship and love and service of the pure and holy angels, the fellowship of the saints of all ages, the unending reunions with the loved ones who have gone on before, ought to inspire every soul to seek for all the fullness of the blessing of the gospel in this life, and at the same time inspire with a lofty and deathless purpose to make sure of realizing all that is offered to us, in time and eternity, through the redemptive work of the Son of God."[36]

What A Challenge

Such prospects are enough to challenge us to persevere in our efforts to develop a character like unto His, regardless of hell's scorns and earth's jeers. In continuing the development of the life of true holiness we must not be satisfied with the defensive—for "the defensive is never a good attitude in warfare with evil. It implies that the most we hope to do is to hold the ground we have. . . . Our religion can never be a religion of the past; it must always be a religion actively present: a religion ever making fresh demands upon us. One feels oftentimes that the trouble with much of our religion is that it has become fossilized in a remote past. Really, a good many people's religion represents an immature stage of development."[37]

Remember that in the crisis of cleansing the aspect of the experience most emphasized there is that of cleansing; but in the continuation of the life beyond the crisis of cleansing, the emphasis should be upon the anointing of the Spirit, the unction from on high, that which gives beauty and fragrance, as well as holy radiance, to the life of the believer who presses for the mark.

With respect to keeping the development of a life of holiness ever before one, I would remind you of the ceremony of Bishops in the Primitive Church. When the Bishop-elect passed before the people they cried out to him: "Remember Eternity! Remember Eternity!" And, so to you as you face the development of this life of holiness, I exhort: "Remember Eternity!"

Chapter Six

True Holiness: Its Practical Aspects
Acts 2:41-47

Previous studies presented the doctrine and the experience of true holiness. But to maintain a proper balance, we must consider the practical life of true holiness. No matter how logical the doctrine may be, nor how accurately the experience may be described, the test question is, "Is it practical? Does it work?"

Some deny that there is such an experience—or that any one can obtain it. But on this all are agreed: Each person who professes holiness is expected to demonstrate it in the daily life. That is reasonable. "We cannot separate experience and practice" in this matter of true holiness. If we do that, and "substitute mere theory, we have but a miserable deformity. He who would have inward experience only is an enthusiast, and he who would have only practice is a Pharisee, and the theorist deals in empty words and speculations. Holiness deals with facts and realities."

The correct blending of doctrine, experience, and life are necessary for proper guidance and proper demonstration of the life of true holiness. Whatever God requires of us is possible by divine aid, reasonable when properly understood, and necessary for God's glory and man's good. An experienced evangelist, the Rev. Foreman Lincicome, expressed it thus: "If one majors on theory and neglects experience and practice, he becomes a formalist. . . . If one majors on experience and neglects theory and practice, he becomes a fanatic. . . . If one majors on practice and neglects theory and experience, he becomes a legalist, or a Pharisee."

The real crux of our struggle in the life of holiness is to ascertain the will of God. Knowing God's will, we must do that, regardless of the cost or consequences to us. Blending the doctrine, experience and life as God's Word teaches it, produces scriptural saints. Let our prayer be: May the Lord make us saints and save us from becoming formalists, fanatics, or Pharisees.

What Is The Difference?

We will do well to consider the fact that "the outward life of the sanctified does not differ from the outward life of the partially sanctified, except it takes on a more intense form. The lowest gracious state turns away from all sin and keeps the commandments of God, and the highest gracious state can do no more. In the advances stages of the religious life, superior light and increased spiritual power enlarge the sphere and intensify religious activities, but do not, properly speaking, either open new spheres or impose new laws of action and effort. There is the same straight gate for all to enter, and the same narrow way for all to walk in. There is not one set of commandments for the feebler, and another for the stronger of God's children, but the same for all."[1]

This life of holiness is on a high plane, but it is consistent with man's limitations. It is for man as he is, since the Fall warped his entire being. The moral nature is cleansed, but the pure nature is resident in the same body, unchanged. The actual transformation is in the moral nature, not the physical. While there is no ethical quality predicable of the body; and "the ethic is in the soul . . . the ethic of the soul is in many ways affected by its relations to the body. . . . The state of the body affects the state of the soul."[2] And the holy soul is left in the same world in which it lived before; that is, "the same environments of all kinds. . . . It is left here to live the common life of humanity itself."[3]

Thus, true holiness does not mean isolation from temptation, or the end of solicitation to evil, accusation by Satan, the removal of human infirmities, and all the trials and tests to which mortals are heirs. "It must go down into the arena and fight with the beasts. Not even the devils are kept aloof from it."[4] But it does mean a practical life of "large ends" and "true purposes." It is a life which outwardly expresses the renovation of the soul. Dr. C. W. Butler declared it to be "God's greatest challenge to the unbelief of a lost world." This life is marked by complete triumph over sin, complete victory persecutions, whether by suspecting brethren or hostile enemies, and by triumph over environments and personalities.

Since it is a life which springs from an inward state of the heat, it is "the most easy, peaceful, and natural life that a human being can live. It is indeed the normal state of man."[5]

While there are those who would emphasize the emotional and ecstatic phases of holiness, we need to appreciate the fact that Mr. Wesley and the early Methodists did not look upon it chiefly "as a feast for the sensibilities," nor "as an insurance policy against the dangers of hell, or a sly passport to heaven." Instead, the life of holiness is to be considered as "a working force . . . a business coat, selected for everyday wear, not for dress parade or state occasions. It is buckled on as the whole armor of God to fight with."[6]

This life is not lived by the motives and energies of this world, but by the motives and energies of the Spirit of God. And one becomes strong when he replaces his strength with the power of the Holy Spirit.

This Is A Life of Purity (Acts 15:8, 9)

This is perfect, personal moral cleansing. "Holiness is freedom from sin. In those once subject to sin, and defiled by sin, it implies the destruction of the reigning power of sin and the washing away of all its pollution. Holiness means victory over sin itself—not merely over the forms of sin."[7]

"The work of salvation is not complete until all sinful tendencies are removed from the soul. For we must clearly distinguish between a sinful tendency and a susceptibility to sin. Without such a susceptibility, man could not be tested. This susceptibility may exist and yet the soul be perfectly sinless. But a sinful tendency is a proneness to sin—an affinity for sin as sin. . . . Unless Jesus Christ can remove all inhering inclinations to sin, He came to do a work which He cannot do. If He cannot take away the carnality which remains after the soul's amicable relations to its maker, He is deficient in the resources needed in a Redeemer of mankind."[8]

This "sin" which is purged is "a virus in the blood and not merely a localized sore."[9] "We are saved from the consequences not only of our past sins, but of a fatal heritage received from the father of our race. . . . For sin is man's worst foe: and none are safely guarded unless they are saved from all sin. . . . Our hearts are emptied of sin by being filled with the Holy Spirit."[10] Holiness is more than purity—which is "a mere negative excellence"—it is "the employment of all our powers and opportunities to work out God's purposes: and this implies the use of our intelligence to learn how best to do His work, and the bodily effort which His work requires."[11]

Purity, then, is a prerequisite for power; for power in impure, selfish, sinful hands would be destructive.

This Is A Life Of Power (Acts 1:8, 2:4)

Many stress the aspect of "power"—and it is there. But it is not power for display purposes. Mountain-moving faith without purity of heart might build a fence about the mountain to be moved, charge an admission fee, and deposit the receipts in its own name.

It is power for holy living. The supreme purpose of holy living is to make us like Christ in every detail of life. It is power to reproduce Christ's holy life.

It is power equal to the responsibility to perform our appointed tasks. Joe Brice tersely reminds us: "The human spirit fails unless the Holy Spirit fills." This means the "re-enactment of Christ's power" which gives victory and makes us "more than conquerors over the world, the flesh, and the devil." "The blessing of holiness is needed to keep alive the aggressive spirit in the Church."

It is the power to influence others for good. The secret of the success of the early Church was the moral power of the Christians. They "turned the world upside down." They were poor, ignorant and obscure; but they were holy in heart and life. "The invincible power" of the early Church and of early Methodism was "that of supreme personal holiness," which is "the unanswerable argument for Christianity."

True holiness means that one imparts to all life a quality which convinces men that true holiness is not something for temples of worship, but that which enriches and ennobles every phase of human life.

This Is A Life Of Spiritual Perception

"This is that . . ." There is glorious enlightenment through the Spirit, Who is to "guide . . . into all truth." Under His illumination veiled truth becomes apparent. This was true in those who experienced the fullness of the Holy Spirit at Pentecost, and manifested itself in that: (1) they had a clearer conception of the plan of salvation, and (2) they understood the essential need of the human heart.

This Spirit-anointed perception saved them from contending over trifles, and taught them what was relevant and vital. Consequently, they put their emphasis on fervent evangelism instead of formal ecclesiasticism. "The argument of logic" gave way to "the appeal of life." "The declaration of a creed" was less important than "the demonstration of a life." Negative repression gave way to positive expression, and this perception produced fragrant fervor and infectious joy.

Understanding God's Program

Their clearer conceptoin of their relation to Christ and His redemptive program (Acts 1:8) gave them the courage to witness in the face of the amazement, scorn, doubt, and ridicule of their fellowmen. Furthermore, they had the courage to correct the popular errors and to rebuke the heinous sins of their countrymen. But even more than that was in evidence, for under the direction of the Spirit, they "challenged the strongholds of sin in the name of the Lord; and undertook a world-encompassing program of evangelism." By shifting from the defensive of complacency to the offensive, they launched a crusade for Christ. The secret was: "Pentecost was a surcharging of human personality with heavenly energy, an infusion of the strength of Christ, an inpouring of impulsive grace, creating a plenitude of ability."[12]

This perception produced a wholesome positiveness. It corrected the vacillation which had previously characterized their lives. Indefiniteness and indifference were banished. Practical piety displaced the "heartless routine of ritualism" with its drift toward pomp, pageantry and priestcraft. Their Spirit-anointed messages pricked men's consciences causing them to cry out: "Men and brethren, what shall we do?" They were quick to detect and resist the subtle encroachments of the secularizing spirit of the world. Their positiveness and enthusiasm produced conviction that could not be easily escaped, because inspired enthusiasm transfigures and enhances personality, making it radiant and irresistible.

This positiveness elevated them to new heights, enabling them to look beyond those fears that harassed their souls, as the fear of poverty, the fear of suffering, the fear of sacrifice, the fear of isolation, the fear of the loss of things, and the fear of criticism from their fellowmen; and looking beyond these things, by faith they saw true values in Christ and His eternal purpose and ample provision for them.

This Is A Life of Persevering Discipleship (Acts 2:41-43)

It was based on a willing reception of God's truth. One is holy only as he wills to be holy. It was continued by conformity of heart and life to the will of God. The sanctified soul has a deep devotion to the will of God, sweetly preferring it to all else in life. It was developed by attention to the apostles' doctrine. We need a teaching ministry today — even as they did in the early Church—which properly blends light (knowledge) and heat (emotion). It was enriched by reverent social association and edification. "He that saith he is in the light, and hateth his brother, is in darkness even until now. He that loveth his brother abideth in the light, and there is none occasion of stumbling in him. But he that hateth his brother is in darkness and walketh in darkness, and knoweth not whither he goeth, because darkness hath blinded his eyes" (I John 2:9-11).

This fellowship was possible because of their character-transformation which made "inmost communion with God" the foremost thing in their lives. When believers are indwelt by the Holy Spirit, and walk in the light, there should be no impediments to fellowship. Sanctity is compatible with the highest and best social privileges and duties. True holiness enriches both personal and public life. Early Methodism undertook to reform the nation by spreading scriptural holiness over the land. Conditions of our day challenge us to go and do likewise.

Its consuming passion is to win souls despite the cost. This explains the early church's self-renunciation and intercession. It is this which beautifies self-denial and community of things. It also glorified their self-sacrifice, as witnesses the result of the martyr and confessor, Stephen, who won a missionary-apostle, Paul.

Barry tells of one who was cultivating this deeper walk with God and was reported to be going insane. When asked for evidence of it, he was told: "He talks religion during office hours."

May God save us from "mild pietism" which is close to "decorous worldliness." We shall find that any profession of discipleship which "does nothing . . . gives nothing . . . costs nothing . . . suffers nothing . . . is worth nothing. . . ." But on the other hand, the "discipleship that costs something, that suffers something, that does something, is always worth something."[13]

This Is Preeminently A Life Of Perfect Love
(I John 4:17, 18—Acts 2:44-47)

Some who advocate the deeper spiritual life seem to overlook that it is a life of love. "Love is the central, animating force in true religion. . . . It is to the soul what blood is to the body. . . . To walk in love, to speak, to act, to purpose, with the love of God pervading all our movements, is the best and sublimest form of existence. To do this, there must be a thorough abnegation of self-will, self-opinion and self-desire."[14] This assures that one loves God supremely and takes a proper attitude toward the will of God. It gives Christ "the preeminence" in all things. This assures that one thinks of self in a proper manner. There is a proper regard for one's self. God respects man's personality, and so should man.

"Not to think more lowly of one's self" than he ought (according to Joseph H. Smith) is as necessary to a properly balanced life as "not to think more highly of himself" than he ought. This guarantees that one loves his brother as himself. "Love is the fulfilling of the law."

Love saves from extremes by assuring a right relationship to God and man. Love compels one to offer freely what selfish ones might call "unnecessary sacrifice." But true holiness produces a love which gives a proper attitude toward one's gifts, talents, possessions, so that love uses all its resources to serve in the best possible way the ultimate good of the greatest number. Love attracts where cold logic repels. The appeal of a Christlike life is like a heavenly cordial to sin-wearied hearts and is rewarded with man's gratitude and God's approving smile. In "such a time as this," we need true holiness—with all its concomitants and consequences. We urgently need what Joe Brice has called the "undying flame of inspired enthusiasm! Religion alight, kindled to white heat, ablaze for God!"

The Modern Reaction to Enthusiasm

We have reached a day when there is intellectual recoil against the emotional expression of one's fervor of soul. "The thought of flaming enthusiasm in religion arouses distrust in the modern mind.... Enthusiasm is permitted in any other pursuit; in religion, it is regarded as bad form. Enthusiasts in piety are either despised as unintelligent zealots or tolerated as well-meaning fanatics. Decorous reserve is the rule in religion; and there are established conventions setting forth what is proper and 'what isn't done.' And yet, New Testament Christianity is holy fire, having little in common with the decorous ritualism which often beggars the name today."[15]

When the soul becomes love-possessed, life takes on a new intensity and formality is removed by the "lambent tongue of flame." True holiness kindles cold obedience into a passion for righteousness and makes "the slavish sense of duty burst into an eager flame of devotion," marking a definite transition from a formal religion to fervent love for the Lord Jesus Christ. This enables one to surmount criticisms from a world that is dead in trespasses and in sins, and ostracism heaped upon him by a Church that is insensitive to spiritual values. If the Church is to mold this generation for God, it must be holy and not worldly, manifesting a new and transcendent piety. You and I must demonstrate our piety by an overmastering enthusiasm regulated by perfect love. Can it be said of us, as it was of the early disciples, that the world "took note of them that they had been with Jesus"?

> "Do we live so close to the Lord today
>   Passing to and fro on life's busy way
> That the world in us can a likeness see
>   To the Man of Calvary?
>
> "Do we love, with love to His own akin
>   All His creatures lost in the mire of sin?
> Will we reach a hand, whatsoe'er it cost
>   To reclaim a sinner lost?
>
> "As an open book they our lives will read
>   To our words and acts giving daily heed;
> Will they be attracted or turn away
>   From the Man of Calvary?"

You may know the theory and sympathize with the experience, but unless you possess the experience and demonstrate the life, you will not lead others into their possibilities in the grace of God. If you know the truth concerning this glorious experience and life of true holiness, yet live beneath your privileges, you are like a doctor who diagnoses the symptoms and prescribes the specific for others but does not himself take the medicine which he knows to be the only cure for the malady.

CHAPTER SEVEN

True Holiness: The Supreme Motive
I Peter 1:15, 16

In previous studies, we considered the philosophy of, the Bible authority for and the nature of the doctrine, the experience and the life of true holiness. Now we shall consider the moral obligation to be holy, or the motives which should cause one to will to be holy. May God help us to be correct and convincing in the study of this glorious and eternally important theme of Motive.

One is distressed to discover that many will agree with his theories and proclamations concerning holiness until he presents it as a positive necessity. Many appreciate hearing of it as their privilege, possible in this life, but they "draw back" and neglect the truth when it is pressed upon them that they are morally obligated to be holy; that holiness is closely knit to the purpose of God for one's life, the glory of God, and the prosperity of His Kingdom.

Holiness Is Imperative

Some look upon holiness as an optional luxury, whereas God's Word presents it as a present imperative, "a positive necessity for entering a holy heaven." Therefore, to neglect this experience, or to reject this truth, is disobedience and sin, which if persisted in involves the loss of the soul. But one should be careful how he presents this truth. Holiness should not be presented in a harsh, driving manner, but with great care to give light on the teaching, and to show that one must have it to maintain uninterrupted communion with God and to be fitted for maximum Christian service here and to have assurance of admission into heaven.

There was a time when it was quite popular to speak flippantly about a second work of grace. Those who did so felt safe in maintaining the first work of grace. The result was that theology suffered a distinct loss, and man is faced with "Cultured humanism" which, with Roman Catholicism, rises to challenge Protestant theology, which Atkinson says "is doomed unless it can discover or recover a doctrine of entire sanctification. It requires a doctrine, and much more, it requires living witnesses without whom no doctrine can arise."[1]

We are ready to admit that any "undue exaltation of a doctrine from its legitimate place is dangerous; the magnifying of any of the parts of a disjointed system is destructive of the whole. But it is also true that any separation of a part from the whole causes incompleteness, destroys the beauty of its proportion and ultimates in disaster."[2] "But holiness of heart is full salvation; it is the climax of the divine procedure, the completion of the work of purification . . ." hence, "the emasculation of experimental holiness from the Christian system is not only destructive of its beauty, but also of its divinity and power."[3] Without holiness, the Christian system is a broken column, a worthless and an impractical scheme. If to give holiness prominence is to blemish the Christian system, to eliminate it is to commit a crime against the system and its Author.

In a matter as vital as this, one must give careful attention to his motives for seeking true holiness. A wrong motive not only prevents one from obtaining that which he seeks; it dishonors God. It is not enough to feel that this is desirable for one's happiness, satisfaction, and usefulness. He must desire it for God's glory—and that alone.

A Binding Requirement

Let us consider some of the motivating factors which obligate man to seek, obtain, and live true holiness. We shall consider first:

The Nature of God

"I am the Lord your God . . . Ye shall be holy: For I, the Lord your God am holy" (Lev. 18:2; 19:2).

"God is holy; and this is the eternal reason why all His people should be holy. . . ."[4] This is "the supreme and all-sufficient reason" which is given for us to be holy, which "underlies the whole superstructure of Christian character" (Dungan). That same author says that the greatest thing in the universe is personality, the greatest thing in personality is character, and the greatest thing in character is love. Then he continues: "The greatest divine project relating to man is character rebuilding, or the restoration of God's full image to the soul of man, the perfecting of the moral nature. And this, being a covenant work, requires the cooperation of man with God's plan, process and purpose."[5]

The holiness of God must not be lightly esteemed. "The holiness of God cannot be contemplated as a distinct attribute of the divine nature, capable of existing by itself, as we may conceive of power, wisdom, omnipresence, or even justice. We can conceive of power without wisdom, or wisdom without power, or of justice without benevolence, for these are all distinct qualities, which may exist each by itself, but we cannot conceive of the holiness of God as capable of existing by itself, but only as pervading every other attribute, and as comprehending every conceivable moral perfection of the divine nature. The holiness of God must be conceived of as embracing every moral quality of the divine nature, comprehending universal rectitude, and entire and absolute moral goodness. . . ."

"As a sentiment or disposition, the holiness of God may be regarded as involving three things:

"(1) An infinite hatred and opposition to sin, or moral evil of every kind and degree. 'Thou art of purer eyes than to behold evil, and canst not look on iniquity . . .' " (Hab. 1:13).

"(2) An infinite love or regard for all that is good and right and holy. This follows as a consequence, for it is not possible to conceive of an intense hatred of wrong, without a corresponding love of what is right. But God has not left us to this inference. 'For the righteous Lord loveth righteousness; his countenance doth behold the upright' (Psalm 11:7). 'For I the Lord love judgment, I hate robbery for burnt offering; . . .' (Isa. 61:8).

"(3) A practical exemplification, and actual communication of goodness, and diffusion of holiness and happiness, so far as is consistent with the law of right, and as can be done in harmony with all the attributes of God, which, as a whole, render Him absolutely and infinitely perfect. Hence, it is that we may read the goodness of God in creation, in Providence and in Redemption; and that in the provision of Grace all has been done that can be done to promote human happiness. God Himself is limited by the immutable perfections of His own nature, in His modes of operation for the redemption of sinners, and the diffusion of holiness and happiness among moral agents."[6]

The will of God is associated with the nature of God as a motive for holiness:
  (1) His will is His desire or wish for His children.
  (2) It is revealed in His commandments: "Be ye holy," etc.
  (3) It is exhibited in Christ's prayer in John 17.
  (4) It is repeated in the apostolic exhortation: "Go on ... perfection."
  (5) It is also reflected in the divine calls: "Called with an holy calling." "Walk before me and be thou perfect."
  (6) Furthermore, His will is demonstrated in His choice for us: "According as He hath chosen us in him before the foundation of the world, that we should be holy and without blame before him in love" (Eph. 1:4).

The permissive will of God is that it is His good pleasure that we be holy; but the authoritative will of God requires and commands us to be holy. And that brings us to consider our relation to God—as "the people for His own possession"—a peculiar people—which morally obligates us to be holy (I Peter 1:15, 16; Titus 2:14).

The Nature of Holiness Is A Motive

A careful examination will reveal that holiness is not a mythical, fanatical something which is contrary to reason —but something reasonable, real, and beautiful, agreeing with the full divine revelation, We see how carefully God has prepared man for a comprehensive understanding of holiness by Old Testament lessons in what one called "the A.B.C. Class of Redemption."

The first idea signifying holiness is that of *Separation*, that which is set apart, or consecrated to sacred uses.

There is a distinction between what is, and what is not, holy; or separated unto—and accepted by—the Lord. *Fitness* enters into this as well as Separation. In Lev. 11:1-8; 19:19, God illustrated this in detail for His people. There were laws forbidding or regulating the use of certain things and animals. Clothing and seed of one kind were not to be mixed with another or divers kind; and clean and unclean animals were to be recognized and God's directions were to be very carefully followed.

The foot and the mouth were to agree. By this agreement, man was enabled to distinguish between the clean and the unclean. Investigation reveals the nature of the creature. In a life that is holy and acceptable, one's walk and talk always agree.

The second idea signifying holiness is that of *Cleanness*. That which is separated, and dedicated to God, must be clean. The purpose of separation is to preserve from defilement. The strictness with which the Levitical economy was enforced reveals the plain fact that God will not accept anything unclean. His right to demand this quality is clearly demonstrated by His own words: "I am the Lord your God . . . I am holy" (Lev. 18:2; 19:2).

The third idea is twofold, embracing the idea of *Wholeness*. This involves *Completeness* and *Soundness*. Holiness is moral wholeness. It is soul symmetry, soul health.

Whatever is to be acceptable to God must be whole, not partial. It must be entire, with none of its parts missing. Furthermore, whatever is acceptable to God must be complete (possessing all its parts)—it must be free from blemishes and defects. Unless it is all there, and all is sound, it is not acceptable (See Lev. 22:17-24.)

Hence out of these lessons, the idea of *moral purity* emerges. Holiness has more than a ceremonial significance. Put all these ideas together—*Separation* (or Dedication)—*Cleanness—Completeness—Soundness*— and one sees very clearly that God was teaching man that He demanded freedom from the corruption and the defilement of sin.

The practical aspect of this is volitional conformity to the will of God, which means love practiced in all our words, thoughts, affections, actions and desires. God has dominion over us as Creator. God has redeemed us from sin's galling yoke by Christ's sacrifice. God has provided us lavishly with all temporal and spiritual blessings, and we ought to reciprocate His love. God increases the capacity for holiness and the enjoyment of holiness in those who conform to His will; therefore, we owe it to Him to conform to His holy and blessed will.

The Nature of Sin Is A Motive for Holiness

To obtain a true picture of holiness, it must be contrasted with its opposite: sin. Nothing could be more unlike than sin and holiness.

One of our perils is that sin shall be considered as a casual, indifferent matter without serious consequences. If man views sin incorrectly, he will also hold incorrect views of holiness. If we view sin correctly, we shall see it as gross inward corruption—a virus of the nature, a rebellion against the authority of God, which leads to the rejection of the Son of God. It defiles that which God created pure. It deranges that which God created orderly and perfect. It debauches man morally and results in the death sentence for the guilty soul (Romans 6:23; James 1:15).

The tragedy is that man is not only infected with a sinful nature, but he also infects others. "By precept and example, he spreads the infernal contagion wherever he goes; joining with the multitude to do evil, strengthening and being strengthened in the ways of sin and death and becoming especially a snare to his own household."[7] Surely from such a condition one would welcome perfect and full salvation.

The Purpose of God Is a Further Motive for Holiness

Not only is holiness the essential nature of God, it is also found to be the purpose of God in creating man in His own image, for "it is the image of God in man that reflects the glory of the divine nature." "Since man's chief end is to glorify God and enjoy Him forever," insofar as he is destitute of this moral likeness to God, man "dishonors God and thwarts the purpose of His being." Therefore, until man is made holy, he cannot perfectly glorify God.

The purpose of God in conducting the universe, in preserving order in this probationary period for man is to promote holiness, to encourage man's quest for it. Thus, it is holiness for this life—or never (Luke 1:75). And should man argue its impossibility, due to an unwholesome environment, he should remember that the God-man, our Redeemer—demonstrated in His earthly life the principles God requires of us in our life. To live holy here may be hard, but it is not impossible if we are identified with Christ (Romans 6:6; John 15:5; Phil. 4:13). In this world, where this image was lost, it is to be restored, ". . . because as He is, so are we in this world" (I John 4:17). The object of Christ's atoning death was our sanctification. "Wherefore Jesus also, that He might sanctify the people with His own blood, suffered without the gate" (Hebrews 13:12). Thus, God is glorified when His Son's mission into the world is accomplished in the destruction of "the works of the devil" in a human heart (I John 3:8); and when Jesus' prayer in John 17 is answered.

The Nature of Christian Service Is Also a Motive

When God created man, it was not only His desire for man to reciprocate His love, which requires holiness; but to serve Him, which also requires holiness: "He hath showed thee, O man, what is good: and what doth the Lord require of thee, but to do justly and to love mercy, and to walk humbly with thy God?" (Micah 6:8). Man's holiness was also the object of the Law and the Gospel (Jer. 31:33; I Tim. 1:5; Rom. 13:10; Matt. 1:21; I John 1:7; and II Peter 1:3, 4). Back of this lies a deeper purpose than to provide man with ecstatic emotions. "The object of all God's promises and dispensations was to bring fallen man back to the image of God, which he had lost. This, indeed, is the sum and substance of the religion of Christ," wrote Adam Clarke.

Our own best interests and usefulness in Christ's work, as well as fitness for it, require personal holiness (Matt. 5:16; Luke 24:49; Acts 1:8). A holy life is a powerful factor in effective work for Christ. Without holiness (1) the worker's fellowship may be intermittent, (2) God's exact messages to His workers may be distorted, (3) there will be a painful consciousness of spiritual deficiency in the workers; and without holiness (4) the worker's spiritual vision is obscured, (5) his spiritual growth is retarded and

(6) his loyalty is challenged by this inner foe, the carnal mind, "which is enmity against God." When we think of the nature of our relation to Christ's Cause, we cannot be indifferent to holiness. A worker can never be any better than his character. "They that bear the vessels of the Lord" must be holy. Therefore, holiness is a necessity for those who are to be effective Christians.

The Nature of Heaven Requires Holiness

By heaven, we mean that state of eternal glory toward which all believers are traveling and for which they are striving in their fight against Satan and sin. Our conception of heaven implies three things:
(1) The absence of all sin, evil, pain and suffering.
(2) The presence of all good, "both of the purest and most exalted kind."
(3) "Complete satisfaction of all the desires of the soul, at all times, and through eternity, without the possibility of decrease on the one hand, or of any termination of the existence of the receiver or the received." This is an inexpressibly glorious state—it is a place, but more. It is a state, but more. It is a state of endless blessedness in the regions of glory, but more: it is God Himself sharing with those who have by His grace been made "heirs of God."

Sin cannot enter heaven, because it is forever excluded. The presence of sin would change the nature of heaven. An unholy man cannot enter into heaven; and were he in it, it would be no enjoyment to him, because it is not suited to him. The nature of the resident must be suited to the place of residence. Therefore, heaven demands holiness of its inhabitants. (See Rev. 21:27.)

Before man enters heaven, he must face death and pass the test of the Judgment; it takes true holiness for these crises (I John 4:17, 18). Holiness gives courage to face the hour of death. Holiness gives confidence in the day of judgment. Man wants holiness for death and the hereafter but God requires it in this life (Heb. 12:14; Matt. 5:8, 48; Luke 1:71-75).

Entrance into heaven with sin in the heart is eternally

impossible (Rev. 21:27). Therefore, God provides it, commands it, and expects it in this life. And since it is necessary for admission into heaven, it is the highest folly to treat it lightly and to be indifferent toward God's call to holiness. Before man faces death and the judgment, there are some sober truths he should ponder:

It is morally impossible for God to create an unholy being.

It is morally impossible for God to approve an unholy being.

It is morally impossible for God to require the impossible of any being.

It is morally impossible for God to provide holiness and require it of man, and then let sin enter heaven.

It is morally impossible for any intelligent and responsible being to reject what Christ provides without rejecting the Christ Who provided it.

Therefore, man's attitude toward holiness is of eternal importance.

"It is often said that we 'cannot be perfect here.' Now, it is true that we cannot in this world reach our full spiritual stature.... It is also true that, as a matter of fact, 'in many things we stumble all' (James 3:2). But it is not at all true that a certain amount of sin is unavoidable. Every sin looked at separately might and ought to have been avoided by the Christian. What is unavoidable cannot be, in the true sense, sin. Much popular language really denies that God's salvation is complete. But this is contrary to the universal teaching of the Scripture (Isaiah 60:21; Jeremiah 31:33, 34; Romans 8:1-5) which assures us that our failures are due not to any incompleteness in the work of salvation on the Divine side, but to our own failure to respond to it (II Cor. 7:1).... God's salvation ever brings the power to obey Him. If we are really unable, we cannot be in a state of salvation at all."[8]

To say then that God's command to be holy is one which it is impossible to obey means, in effect, that those who hold that position do so because of a "choice in attitudes" rather than through conclusions reached after "an accumulation of facts." To deny the possibility of holiness in this life means that one's attitude toward sin is more cordial than toward the scriptural facts and convincing arguments that salvation delivers from all sin.

Try as man may, he can never escape the claims of true holiness. Bishop Foster once wrote:

"In the university of heaven, whose president is God, and whose catalog is the Bible, the course of study is plainly laid down. We may say without fear of successful contradiction that God's Word has majored on holiness! It breathes in the prophecy, thunders in the law, murmurs in the narrative, whispers in the promises, supplicates in the prayers, sparkles in the poetry, resounds in the songs, speaks in the types, glows in the imagery, voices in the language and burns in the spirit of the whole scheme, from Alpha to Omega, from its beginning to its end. Holiness!

"Holiness required, holiness offered, holiness attainable, holiness a present duty, a present privilege, a present enjoyment, is the progress and completeness of its wondrous theme. It is the truth glowing all over, welling all through revelation, the glorious truth which sparkles and whispers and sings and shouts in all its history, and biography, and poetry, and prophecy and precept and promise and prayer, the great central truth of Christianity."[9]

And the human soul, in its quest for the fullest divine provision for its deepest inner need, cries out:

> "O for that flame of living fire,
> Which shone so bright in saints of old;
> Which bade their souls to heav'n aspire,
> Calm in distress, in danger bold.
>
> Where is that Spirit, Lord, which dwelt
> In Abrah'm's breast, and sealed him Thine?
> Which made Paul's heart with sorrow melt,
> And glow with energy divine?
>
> That Spirit which from age to age
> Proclaimed Thy love and taught Thy ways?
> Brightened Isaiah's vivid page,
> And breathed in David's hallowed lays?
>
> Is not Thy grace as mighty now
> As when Elijah felt its power;

When glory beamed from Moses' brow,
Or Job endured the trying hour?

Remember, Lord, the ancient days;
Renew Thy work; Thy grace restore;
And while to Thee our hearts we raise,
On us Thy Holy Spirit pour."

To reject this provision after being convinced of its possibility and imperative necessity will surely jeopardize one's standing with God. No degree of success justifies any degree of disobedience. To refuse this experience is a sin against the God Who designs it, the Christ Who provides it, the Spirit Who effects it, the Church which needs it, as well as your own soul and the souls of others.

CHAPTER EIGHT

True Holiness: Some Duties, Difficulties, Dangers, and Distinctions

True holiness has been presented as (1) a valid Bible doctrine to be believed; (2) a vital personal experience to be received; and (3) a victorious Spirit-filled life to be lived. Such a life has been described as "God's greatest challenge to a lost world." It is one thing to give mental assent to the doctrine. It is another thing to personally seek and obtain the experience of a pure heart. Once the experience is received there must be positive effort to maintain and demonstrate the sanctified life.

Satan will do everything he can to perplex and mislead those who seek to "wholly follow the Lord." If he cannot gain "entrance through a direct avenue of the heart [he] will indirectly venture by way of a confused brain."[1]

The doctrine of holiness has been set forth more fully, in general, than have the duties, difficulties, dangers, and the necessary distinctions in the cultivation of the sanctified life. Harry E. Jessop described the effect of such neglect as: "They never wavered in their fundamentalism, but they dried up in their spiritual experience."[2]

Dr. A. W. Tozer wrote of some who "set forth correctly the principles of the doctrine of Christ, [who] minister constantly to believers who feel within their breasts a longing which their teaching simply does not satisfy."[3] He continued, "The whole transaction of religious conversion has been made mechanical and spiritless. Faith may now be exercised without a jar to the moral life and without embarrassment to the Adamic ego. Christ may be received without creating any special love for Him in the soul of the receiver. The man is 'saved,' but he is not hungry or thirsty after God. In fact, he is specifically taught to be satisfied and encouraged to be content with little."[4]

It is suggested that one reason for a "lack of interest in personal holiness" may be "a disproportionate emphasis in fundamentalism on the work of God *for* man, rather than *in* man; positional sanctification rather than on practical salvation."[5] A life of true holiness is not impossible to man during his earthly sojourn. It is God's will for man in this present life. The greatest Example of personal holiness is the Lord Jesus Christ. He was very man and "was in all points tempted like as we are, yet without sin" (Heb. 4:15). Thus "He is able to succour them that are tempted" (Heb. 2:18). We are to "follow His steps" (I Peter 2:21).

Christians are obligated to study in order to be "approved unto God, a workman that needeth not to be ashamed, rightly dividing the word of truth" (II Timothy 2:15). God-approved workmen will set the "standard" of life and conduct where God's Word sets it: not higher, thus causing many to despair of obtaining a pure heart and living a holy life; nor do they place it lower, thereby causing both the doctrine and the life of holiness to be held in disrepute.

Duties of the Sanctified Life

Associate with those who think and believe as you do concerning the truth. "They that feared the Lord spake often one to another" (Mal. 3:16a).

Immediately begin to study the Bible, measuring your experience and life by its teachings. You will find that this life is like a beautiful and unique mansion with its many rooms awaiting your discovery.

Be ready to share your testimony at the proper time, and in a proper manner. "Be ready always to give an answer to every man that asketh you a reason of the hope that is in you with meekness and fear" (I Peter 3:15).

Avoid argument. Those who love to argue are often the least apt to be reached by debate. "Let your speech be alway with grace, seasoned with salt, that ye may know how ye ought to answer every man" (Col. 4:6).

Keep your Christian life balanced and practical. Holiness is a superior experience and a practical life. (See Romans 12 and I Cor. 12:31b-13:13). Maintain care to keep your life within proper bounds. Avoid stressing your experience to the point where it might repel some who *would* be won by the display of a "symmetrical whole" life. "Holiness is not merely an internal experience of cleansing and ecstasy; it is an external expression of the same in which Christ is witnessed in the smallest and most insignificant actions of the daily life. Unless one's outer life . . . is a genuine counterpart of the Christ-life within, our holiness is a defective thing."[6]

It is the duty of the sanctified to maintain the conditions by which this experience was obtained. That involves "a perpetual and entire devotement of yourself to Him, with a faith as perfect and undoubting. . . . Our aim in the justified life was to obtain perfect deliverance from sin; now it ought to be to 'be preserved blameless and presented faultless.' That is God's part conditioned on our faithful performance of our own part of the work."[7]

Another duty of the sanctified person is to *avoid everything doubtful*, being constantly on the alert for new light. The Holy Spirit is a faithful Guide to all who are completely abandoned to the will of God. (See John 16:13.) There may be times when one will be confronted by things called "no harm." Then one faces a critical decision. Be careful, for Satan seeks to gain advantage by using one of his "entering wedges." In such a dilemma remember what has been called "the railway rule": *"In case of doubt, take the safe side."* That is a safe guide for the Christian life because "under the influence of the Spirit, it is impossible to decide against God's will without doubt."[8] Doubt about a thing may be God's challenge to delay a decision for further prayer and counsel.

As we "walk in the light," our capacity for light concerning ourself and the truth of God increases. New light does not mean that the work God wrought in the heart was superficial. "The true test of the genuineness of the work is our perfect willingness, without controversy and hesitation, to follow all the light God gives us. Perfect purity is demanded in the motives and not perfect wisdom in our life. Consequently, we must seek continually to secure greater light."[9]

Difficulties of the Sanctified

The life of the sanctified is most blessed. Some consider it to be one of constant ecstasy, where one always *feels* like singing about Beulah land where "the milk and honey" flows unceasingly. They are surprised to learn that after entering into this spiritual Canaan-land experience, there is a Jericho and an Ai to be subdued. (Read Joshua, chapters 1-7.)

Some of our difficulties arise from within, others are from without. To properly determine their origin requires careful study and prayer. One has warned against the difficulty of "the ill-advised extravagances by following sudden, untested impressions."[10] Those who desire to cultivate deep spirituality seem to be Satan's special targets. On the subject of *Impressions*, one especially helpful book[11] has been reprinted. An especially helpful treatment of problems arising from within has been prepared by two scholarly representatives of the Wesleyan-Arminian position. Its study will prove to be most helpful.[12]

Further difficulties may arise out of errors in judgment. A clean heart is no assurance that one will not err in judgment. John Wesley's emphasis was on perfection of motive or intention, not perfection of the intellect. One may be wrong in his judgment, yet perfect in his motive. "Keep thy heart with all diligence; for out of it are the issues of life" (Prov. 4:23).

Another area of difficulties is that of the different personalities of the sanctified. Since the Creator made "one star" to differ "from another star" (I Cor. 15:41), one should not be surprised to find that there are variations in human personalities. Some may be due to environment, some to one's background, some to personal capacities and training, and some may be due to the beliefs and practices of those who led them to the Lord. The point at issue is not the *fact* of such differences, but *how* the sanctified react to those differences. The pattern for all to follow is set forth in Paul's Epistle to the Romans, chapter 14, and in his First Epistle to the Corinthians who had some very real differences to face. Love was the solvent for their problem. (See I Cor. 13.) The Christian life may hold many and varied difficulties, but God has the grace and power to enable the determined Christian's life to be "a constant pageant of triumph" (II Cor. 2:14; 4:8-15).

Dangers of the Sanctified

Do not be shocked to discover that the life of the sanctified person is beset by dangers. Overlooking that fact gives Satan an advantage in his attacks.

Dr. Joseph Owen wrote: "Those in possession of this 'like precious faith' should be warned of the Dangers, instructed as to the Differences, and taught concerning the Difficulties of the sanctified life."[13]

It is essential to keep in mind "three facts distinct in Christian experience; namely, spiritual life, moral purity, and Christian maturity. Spiritual life is received in regeneration; moral purity, in sanctification; while Christian maturity is the result of growth in grace. Regeneration is a gift; sanctification is an act; maturity is a process.... Purity is an obtainment; maturity is an accumulation."[14]

Since the sanctified experience itself "must be tested under probationary conditions—lived in a human environment of limitations and frailty, and in a world environment that is neither 'friend of grace to help us on to God,' nor a support of grace to keep us with God,"[15] it becomes necessary to indicate some of the dangers which may be encountered by the sanctified.

One danger is considering purity of heart as the goal, whereas it is "fitness" for life and service on earth, as well as fitness for Heaven. Purity is the foundation of character. Consider the words of Adam Clarke on Eph. 3:19: "To be filled with God is a great thing; to be filled with *the fullness* of God is still greater; to be filled with *all the fullness* of God is greatest of all. This utterly bewilders the sense and confounds the understanding by leading at once to consider the immensity of God, the infinitude of his attributes, and the absolute perfection of each."[16]

The saintly Fletcher described this fulness as "a state of grace beyond sanctification. Sanctification does not graduate the believer in God's love. It only conditions him to advance in that love." In fact, we just begin to develop and grow after we are sanctified.

Another danger is that of misplaced emphasis. One of the spiritual giants in the holiness movement a generation ago warned against what he called losing the "force" (or power) through compromise, and losing the "field" (or following) through misplaced emphasis. One must constantly guard against the imbalance between the devotional life and the practical life. One's "behavior" must precede his "do-havior." Personal character determines the nature of one's conduct.

One must also guard against constantly shifting the emphasis so that folk are more conversant with what one opposes than what he favors, or *why* he opposes or favors those things. It may be easier to denounce the so-called negatives than to defend one's scriptural reasons for opposing them and for favoring the positive. Both the positive and the negative are necessary.

A godly bishop is quoted as saying: "If we lift truth out of its proper proportion and unduly stress a minor truth at the expense of a major truth, we hinder the whole range of truth, for truth is a unit. Truth is symmetrical, and if we emphasize a lesser truth, we spoil the symmetry of the whole."[17] May God help us to avoid losing either our "force" or our "field."

Another very real danger is allowing outward appearance to substitute for inward reality. It seems much easier to make the outward, visible aspects of life conform to a popular pattern, than to submit to the Holy Spirit's requirements for the inward approval of conformity to the whole will of God.

Dr. L. R. Dunn described this danger thus: "There may be amiability of disposition, and a heart as cold and dead toward God as a flinty rock. There may be a temperance of habits, and the constant utterance of blasphemies. There may be suavity of manners, with all the slavish patterns of libertinism. There may be honesty in dealing with our fellowmen, while our hearts by pride, or unbelief, or indifference, or rebellion, may be robbing God of the honor and glory due unto Him. There may be benevolence toward suffering humanity, and be the basest ingratitude toward God."[18]

Closely associated with that danger is presuming that material prosperity indicates spiritual growth. Remember, one may lose "the force" while gaining "the field." (See Matt. 16:26.) It takes the "wisdom from above" (James

3:17) and the power of the Holy spirit to resist the encroachment of the spirit of the world. (Read I John 2:15-17.) One must keep sensitive to the checks and the promptings of the Holy Spirit to detect the suggestions of Satan in an age characterized by secularism. (See Heb. 4:12; 5:14.)

"The loss of the ideal of Christian perfection as the crown of a Spirit-possessed life is symbolized by the virtual disappearance of the term 'saint' from our vocabulary.... The dominant ideal of character in recent generations has been that of the congenial, sociable, adjusted person who pleases everybody but lack moral principles and spiritual depth."[19]

Furthermore, there is the danger of indulging in judging, name-calling and labeling, evils which have done untold harm. It is true that "by their fruits ye shall know them" (Matt. 7:16-20). But He who spoke those words had previously said, "Judge not, that ye be not judged" (Matt. 7:1). Some who insist that their judgment *is* based on "fruits" may not themselves be perfect examples of the "fruit of the Spirit" (Gal. 5:22, 23). Even genuine fruit may lack what Dr. George D. Watson referred to as "October mellowness." It behooves each one to endeavor "to keep the sweet juices of perfect love from souring"; and to avoid criticism of those who may be slow in accepting our convictions on some things. Remember I Cor. 13.

The *"self family"* is the source of dangers. There may be self-deception by rushing into a hasty profession of holiness, which may be both superficial and incomplete due to a lack of understanding of the conditions to be met. In some instances, it may be recovery from a backslidden state.

Self-confidence is a very real danger. Holiness is a great experience, and Satan may subtly tempt one to trust in self for security. "The very thought of safety puts one off . . . guard completely, and makes room for spiritual onslaught."[20]

There is also the danger of self-satisfaction, which may arise out of the unwitting mistake of considering this glorious experience as the end (or goal) of salvation, rather than the means of salvation. Stephan reminds that wonderful as this experience is, "it is only a starting point to infinite lengths ahead, a new departure in growth, knowledge, energy and usefulness in service. How easy it is to ... conclude that we have reached the climax. ... We are not completed, boxed and addressed to the glory world with nothing to do but shout all the way. There is work for us to do."[21]

Some Necessary Distinctions

As a scriptural background for this section of the study, read I Cor. 14:7-12 and II Timothy 2:15. Note the necessity for proper determination of the distinctive qualities of the terms employed. Just as there is a characteristic difference between *good* and *evil*, and *thrift* and *avarice*, we should observe carefully the terminology used in this section of the study. We shall endeavor to use commonly-understood terms instead of technical terms.

It will be helpful at this point to distinguish between the *Christian Perfection* advocated by Wesleyan-Arminians and the *"Perfectionism"* often used by those of other schools of theological thought who dispute the possibility of obtaining Christian perfection in this life. Illustrative of the "perfectionism" we do not teach is a booklet by an outstanding Christian psychologist.[22] The Wesleyan-Arminian theological position on Christian Perfection is clearly set forth in two articles: one by Dr. Don Bastian and the other by Bishop Leslie Marston.

In his article, Dr. Bastian cited the five points of Arminianism: "(1) God wants to save all men. ... (2) Christ died for all men. ... (3) Mankind is corrupted by sin or totally depraved, but God extends to every man a grace which enables him to turn to Christ for forgiveness. This is called Prevenient Grace—the grace that goes before. (4) Because man is truly a free moral agent, he may, if he chooses, resist the grace of God. This is termed Resistible Grace. ... (5) Because man does not surrender this freedom when he is saved, he is able (though less likely than some preachers imply) to renounce his faith and be lost. Arminius was of the conviction that all men are free moral agents both before and after they are converted." Dr. Bastian concluded his article: "An Arminian is one who believes that

God, in Christ, extends His love to all men and that each one must accept personal responsibility for his attitude toward that love."[23]

Bishop Marston, after discussing the "efforts of Pelagian rationalism to corrupt Arminianism," presented the Wesleyan phase of the subject. "We may say that Wesleyanism is original Arminianism baptized with the Holy Spirit. Thus the Methodist movement restored and vivified Arminianism."

Bishop Marston, in considering "the three channels of doctrine in this day that as intelligent and sincere Christians, we should carefully distinguish"; and citing *"Liberal Arminianism"* and *"Neo-Calvinism,"* he described *"Wesleyan Arminianism,* which is the original Arminian doctrine infused with the warmth of the Holy Spirit. It opposes the Pelagianism of liberalism by its insistence upon the necessity of a Redeemer because of man's historic fall and his present sins, and opposes the Antinomianism of Calvinism by maintaining the doctrine of deliverance from the taint of inbred depravity and grace to enable man to live without wilful sinning."[24]

Apropos these doctrinal distinctions, we need to heed Bishop Marston's three suggestions: *"First,* let us remember that in both groups may be found some who are better than their doctrines require and who may indeed be Christian in life. *Second,* while graciously tolerant of those who believe another doctrine, let us remember that in the long run, what we believe will powerfully influence our lives; and to guard against the errors of others, let us seek to understand clearly our own doctrines and their grounding in Scripture. *Third,* let us live up to our doctrines so that our lives and our radiant Christian experience will carry conviction to our friends that a pure heart and life are indeed provided by God's abundant grace and can be maintained by the indwelling of the Holy Spirit."[25]

The relationship of the crisis experience and the development of the entirely sanctified life has been treated in earlier chapters of this book. Those who wish to pursue that phase of the subject will find much help in one of Dr. T. M. Anderson's books, *After Sanctification.*[26]

There must be a proper distinction between human

feelings and the *will.* Our feelings, or sensibilities, are a vital part of our personality, along with the intellect and the will. (See I Peter 1:3-9.) Kagawa used "the economy of feeling" to describe the area in which most people seem to live: the emotional life. There is an emotional aspect to the sanctified life, but one must guard against undue attention to feelings and neglect of the will. The Bible refers to the joys of a "life hid with Christ in God," but places emphasis upon the human will. (See Matt. 6:10; Acts 21:14; James 4:15; Rom. 1:10; Phil. 2:13; John 7:17; Matt. 23:37.) To will involves more than inclination or tendency.

To live a holy life demands one's entire commitment to do the whole will of God. Commissioner Samuel L. Brengle of the Salvation Army was quoted as saying that sanctification as a conscious Christian experience is characterized by changes, but as a state of moral purity, it never fluctuates while the soul abides in Christ. More than 50 years after his crisis experience of entire sanctification, someone asked Brengle if he had experienced changes or vacillations. His reply was: "Judging by the emotions, yes; but by the volition, No!" There never was a time when he willed to be separated from God's will, but there were times when his feelings (or emotions) fluctuated. A case in point is the time he was struck on the head by a brick tossed from a crowd to whom he was preaching. It necessitated hospitalization and a long convalescence. Out of that experience came his book, *Helps to Holiness,* which helped many into the blessing. His assessment of that experience was: "No brick, no book! No book, no blessing! Thank God for the brick that brought the book, that brought blessing to so many!"

An entirely sanctified person may not only know when he is misunderstood, misrepresented, and mistreated, but may be so deeply pained that tears flow because of it. The removal of the carnal mind makes one more sensitive to events that affect the spirit. The indwelling Holy Spirit enables one's reactions to reflect "the fruit of the Spirit" instead of "the works of the flesh" (Gal. 5:19-26). True holiness does not destroy one's feelings, but gives control over them.

Well-intentioned persons have often referred to a sanctified person being as "dead" to hurts and insults as something inanimate. That is an improper comparison because the object never possessed the characteristics of a person: intellect, sensibility and will. The sanctified soul is "dead indeed unto sin, but alive unto God through Jesus Christ our Lord" (Rom. 6:11). That is the assurance that by faith in God's promises and power, his life may be "a constant pageant of triumph in Christ" (II Cor. 2:14, Moffatt).

It is also very necessary to make a careful and clear distinction between *temptation* and *sin*. Some mistakenly think that the sanctified are freed from temptation. But God's people are a tested and tried people. (Read Daniel 12:10; James 1:12; I Peter 4:12.) The Son of God "suffered being tempted" (Heb. 2:18) "in all points like as we are, yet without sin" (Heb. 4:15). See also Matt. 4:1-11.

Bear in mind that the word translated "temptation" is also said to mean testing, severe trial, put under severe pressure, to prove, etc. The early Christians certainly had trials, tribulations and temptations. By the grace and power of God, despite their tribulations, they entered into the Kingdom of God (Acts 14:22).

Subjection to temptation is a fact of life. Words could be multiplied, but Stephan stated the truth succinctly: "It may seem very strange to some that the very life that proposes to give the soul security is one fraught with danger. . . . As long as there is a devil, and man is a free moral agent, there will be danger, it matters not what state of grace one is in. Temptation has assailed the immaculate Son of God and certainly will assail the best of us, who, as long as we live, are liable to fall, as the power to sin is an attribute of free and responsible creatures. This made it possible for our first parents to fall; it was this which put conditionality in the state of angels and allowed them to fall; and this it is which makes fate tremble all through life. While the experience of sanctification does not save us from this possibility, it does lessen the probability of falling. The faculty or power to sin remains, but the desire to sin is destroyed, and thus continues as long as we rest entirely on the power of God. It is certain that no one ever fell while living a life of faith and fully committing themselves to their Preserver."[27]

Temptation is necessary for the development of Christian character. The difference to remember is that sin lies in yielding to the temptation. It is very important, however, to understand the source of the temptation. The carnal nature is the source of temptation to the unsanctified. The sanctified will find some temptations coming through the natural appetites[28] and biological drives which "are not eradicated from the sanctified, they are only kept pure."[29]

The "process of temptation," in the sense of solicitation to evil, may begin with a simple thought of evil, which is followed by a strong impression upon the imagination by the thing presented. This may produce delight in viewing it, thus creating a desire for it. The next step is the consent of the will to perform. It is at the point of "the consent of the will," when desire "hath conceived, it bringeth forth sin; and sin, when it is finished, bringeth forth death" (James 1:12-15).

"The temptation that leads astray may be as sudden as it is successful. We may lose in one moment the fruit of a whole life. . . . To know when to fight, and when to fly, is of great importance to the Christian life. . . . 'resist the first overtures of sin,' is a good maxim. After remedies come too late."[30]

There are two sides to temptation: Satan's solicitation with the downward drag; and God's challenge to do otherwise, thus turning the contest into triumph for God "to the praise of His glory." For instance, Satan's temptation to lie is a challenge to be truthful. The Satanic temptation to indulge "the flesh" is an opportunity to maintain purity of heart and life. Temptation to be selfish offers the opportunity to display unselfishness. The list could be continued *ad infinitum*. The way to defeat the adversary of the soul is by "the sword of the Spirit, which is the Word of God" (Eph. 6:17; Matt. 4:4, 7, 10).

An English author presented a very pertinent article on "Wesley's Well-Balanced Views Regarding Sin." In the article, he seeks to show "the moral and spiritual condition of a Christian made perfect in love . . . living amid surroundings most inimical to its continued existence, but . . . Divine grace . . . so far prevails that every motion of their being tends only to show forth the glory of God's power and truth and love. The conflict with sin rages louder than ever. . . .

"Wesley's view of the state of an entirely sanctified Christian might be illustrated by analogy from a telephone exchange in a besieged city. In the city are several persons known to be friendly to the enemy, and the orders of the exchange operators are, not to give these any connections whatever with the others over the telephone system. Accordingly, when one of them rings up the exchange to get into connection with someone else, he is told the connection cannot be made, and his every attempt stops dead at the exchange. This is effected, not by destroying any part of the exchange apparatus, but by having a loyal telephone operator working it. The figure will speak for itself, if that loyal operator be taken as representing the spirit of a Christian in whose heart Christ now reigns supreme and alone."[31]

It is also vitally important to discern the distinction between *infirmities and sins.* Entire Sanctification cleanses the heart from sin, but it does not remove the infirmities from the life. Vine declares the literal meaning of the word translated "infirmities" to be "want of strength . . . weakness, inability to produce results."[32]

The problem of infirmities and sins arises over the practice of some theologians "all of whom so crudely confound the carnal nature within the believer with the essential human nature that they fail to distinguish between the things which vitally differ."[33]

John Wesley, in describing Christian Perfection, said: "The highest perfection which man can attain while the soul dwells in the body, does not exclude ignorance and error and a thousand other infirmities. Now, from wrong judgments, wrong words and actions will often necessarily flow: And in some cases, wrong affections also may spring from the same source. I may judge wrong of you. I may think more or less highly of you than I ought to think: and this mistake in my judgment may not only occasion something wrong in my behaviour, but it may have a still deeper effect: it may occasion something wrong in my affection. From a wrong apprehension, I may love and esteem you either more or less than I ought. Nor can I be freed from a liableness to such a mistake, while I remain in a corruptible body. A thousand infirmities, in consequence of this, will attend my spirit, till it returns to God who gave it."[34]

In Sermon 82 on *Temptation*, Wesley spoke very clearly on "the nature of that body with which your soul is connected." He said: "Consider... the present state of the soul as long as it inhabits the house of clay. I do not mean in its unregenerate state;... under the dominion of the prince of darkness.... See those who have tasted that the Lord is gracious. Yet still how weak is their understanding! How limited its extent! How confused, how inaccurate, are our apprehensions of even the things that are round about us. How liable are the wisest of men to mistake! to form false judgments;—to take falsehood for truth, and truth for falsehood; evil for good, and good for evil! What starts, what wanderings of imaginations, are we continuously subject to! And how many are the temptations which we have to expect even from these innocent infirmities!"[35]

Wesley warned "those that fear God," to guard against the perils of dwelling "in the ruins of a disordered world, among men that know not God." He also warned that "those that are *perfected in love*"... "even those who 'stand fast in the liberty wherewith Christ has made them free,' who are now really perfect in love, may still be an occasion of temptation to you; for they are still encompassed with infirmities. They may be dull of apprehension; they may have a natural heedlessness, or a treacherous memory; they may have too lively an imagination: And any of these may cause little improprieties, either in speech or behaviour, which though not sinful in themselves, may try all the grace you have: Especially if you impute to perverseness of will (as it is very natural to do) what is really owing to defect of memory, or weakness of understanding:—if these appear to you to be voluntary mistakes, which are really involuntary. So proper was the answer which a saint of God (now in Abraham's bosom) gave me some years ago, when I said, Jenny, surely now your mistress and you can neither of you be a trial to the other, as God has saved you both from sin! 'O, Sir,' said she, 'if we are saved from sin, we still have infirmities enough to try all the grace that God hath given us!' "[36]

Those quotations from Mr. Wesley confirm the *need* for a proper distinction between infirmities and sins. To err at that point subjects the believer to one of two perils: On one hand, we may unnecessarily "blame and afflict ourselves;" and on the other hand, we may incorrectly "excuse ourselves from blame when we are really culpable." Keep in mind Wesley's concept of sin: "A voluntary transgression of a known law of God." Silcox, quoted in *The Biblical Illustrator,* declared: "There is a wide difference between an infirmity and a sin. Sin is the deliberate choice of wrong.... Failure may arise from an inherent weakness or ignorance."

To these words let us add those of the saintly John Fletcher: "An infirmity has its foundation in involuntary want of power; and a sin is a wilful use of the light and power we have."[37]

The infirmities of the sanctified were referred to by Mr. Wesley as "a thousand nameless defects." They are as varied as the individuals. It may be helpful to consider Joseph H. Smith's suggested classification of infirmities as (1) Physical, (2) Mental, (3) Emotional, (4) Spiritual, and (5) Social.

Under *physical*, those related to the body, may be included the normal, God-constituted appetites for food, drink, sex ("biological drives"), exhaustion, fatigue, sleep, etc. Under *mental*, those related to the mind, may be listed lapses of memory, errors of judgment regarding persons and values, inexact appraisals of situations, too lively an imagination; lack of balance between excitability and apathy, cheerfulness or despondency, courage or timidity; wandering thoughts; and *thoughts of evil* thrust into the mind by Satan, as distinct from *evil thoughts* which result from wilful intrusion into the area of forbidden thinking; and difficulty in making decisions.

Emotional infirmities include fear of danger; excessive feelings of grief, sorrow; annoyance at the unpunctuality of others, lack of balance, etc. It is obvious that only a few of the "thousand other infirmities" of which Mr. Wesley spoke, can be cited in any category.

Under *spiritual* infirmities, those associated with our relationship to God, might be included the inability to properly reflect the inward feelings in public or private witness for the Lord, or in public prayer; righteous indignation, unwisely expressed; and distress over lack of progress in achieving one's spiritual goals may be embarrassing infirmities.

Respecting *social* infirmities, which relate to our association with our fellowmen, their "name is Legion for [they] are many." Only a few are suggested, such as annoying idiosyncrasies (habits, mannerisms, mode of expression peculiar to an individual; personal oddity, etc.). One has described such persons, however well intentioned they are, as those who "rub the fur the wrong way" without apparent awareness (or care?) that they may be doing so. There are "grace-helpers," but these seem to be "grace-testers." Their motives are good, but their methods are not recommended.

A constant question is: Why are the sanctified subjected to infirmities? Obviously because they are members of a fallen race. Although redemption from sin has been adequately provided for the soul during this life (Luke 1:67-75), in God's plan, *all things* are not yet completely redeemed. The body, the mind, the emotional nature, which bear "the scars of sin," as one has called the infirmities, indeed "the whole creation groaneth and travaileth in pain together until now. And not only they, but ourselves also ... even we ourselves grown within ourselves, waiting for the adoption, to wit, the redemption of our body" (Romans 8:22). Paul's great classic on the resurrection of the body (I Cor. 15) reveals the glories of that resurrection for which we wait. In Rev. 21:5, John relays God's declaration of the Divine purpose to "make all things new." Then redemption will have been completed. For that day, our hearts are yearning!

There are logical reasons for the infirmities of the sanctified. They keep one humble, free from self-gratification over personal achievements in the Lord's work. After all, we are "unprofitable servants" when "we have done that which was our duty to do" (Luke 17:10).

They teach moment-by-moment dependence upon the atoning blood of Christ. Any lack of perfect conformity to the Divine pattern calls for the atoning blood of Christ. Mr. Wesley's understanding was that *involuntary* action was *not* sin, properly so-called, and that as long as one walked "in the light as he is in the light ... the blood of Jesus Christ his Son cleanseth us from all sin" (I John 1:7).

Furthermore, infirmities teach *sympathy with, and tolerance for, others* who are troubled with infirmities even as we are. There may be some who never speak of their infirmities, but they yearn for understanding and support from someone with whom they could share their burden. If and when another confides in you, bury that confidence in your heart, and speak of it only to God in prayer. Share the burden, not increase it! Remember that *your* infirmities may be as great a trial to others as theirs are to you.

We must be ever-watchful lest Satan gain advantage over us by the human element. Our Savior who took upon Himself "the form of a servant, and was made in the likeness of men" (Phil. 2:7), and "was in all points tempted like as we are, yet without sin" (Heb. 4:15) shows us that humanness is not a barrier to holiness.

Although God's Word makes a clear distinction between infirmities and sins, Satan has used the infirmities of the sanctified to cause many to conclude that it is impossible to live holy while "dwelling in earthly tabernacles." Those desiring further help on the matter are referred to Daniel Steele's articles on this subject.[38]

The Perfection advocated by Wesleyan-Arminians is not Absolute perfection, Angelic perfection, Adamic perfection, nor Resurrection perfection; but perfection of love, perfection of intention and motive. Dr. Steele says that "infirmities are failures to keep the *law of perfect obedience* given to Adam in Eden. This law no man on earth can keep, since sin has impaired the powers of universal humanity. Sins are offenses against the law of love, the *law of Christ,* which is epitomized by John ... (I John 3:23). ... Refusal to love with the whole heart is the ground of condemnation, and not inevitable failures in keeping the law of Adamic perfection."[39]

"Infirmities are an involuntary outflow from our imperfect moral organization. Sin is always voluntary. ... Infirmities have their ground in our *physical nature* and they are aggravated by *intellectual deficiencies.* But sin roots itself in our *moral* nature, 'springing either from the habitual corruption of our hearts, or from the unresisting perversion of our tempers.' "[40]

"Infirmities entail regret and humiliation. Sin always produces guilt. Infirmities in well-instructed souls do not interrupt communion with God. Sin cuts the telegraphic communication with heaven. *The Infirmities of unenlightened believers, being regarded as sins, may produce condemnation by destroying confidence in God.* Thousands are in this sad condition."[41] (Emphasis added.)

Concerning infirmities of which we are not aware, "they are covered by the blood of Christ without a definite act of faith, in the case of a soul vitally united with Him. . . . (Hebrews 9:7). Sins demand a special personal resort to the blood of sprinkling and an act of reliance on Christ."[42]

By the keeping power of Christ, sins are avoidable. But we are subject to infirmities so long as we are in the body. "Jude understood the distinction between faults, or infirmities, and sins [verse 25]. In his scheme of Christian perfection faults are to disappear in the life to come, but we are to be saved from ours sins now."[43]

In Psalm 19:12, 13, David makes a distinction between "unconscious faults" and "known wilful sin." John Wesley repeatedly declared: "Nothing is sin, strictly speaking, but a voluntary transgression of a known law of God."[44]

In a matter of such importance as the distinction between infirmities and sins, one must carefully guard against error. "Though a well-meant mistake does not defile the conscience and bring it into condemnation, nevertheless when discovered it demands a penitent confession and a presentation of the great sin-offering unto the God of absolute holiness. The refusal to do this after the sin offering has been provided involves personal guilt."[45]

At this very point, Mr. Wesley wrote: "(1) not only sin properly so-called (that is, a voluntary transgression of a known law), but sin, improperly so called, (that is, an involuntary transgression of a divine law, known or unknown) needs the atoning blood. (2) I believe there is no such perfection in this life as excludes these involuntary transgressions which I apprehend to be naturally consequent on the ignorances and mistakes inseparable from mortality. . . . (4) I believe a person filled with the love of God is still liable to these involuntary transgressions. (5) Such transgressions you may call sins, if you please: I do not, for the reasons above-mentioned."[46]

May the prayerful and careful study of this distinction give a proper appreciation of Jesus' words in the Model

Prayer as recorded in Matt. 6:10 and Luke 11:4; and of Charles Wesley's words in his hymn, "Every moment, Lord, I want [need] the merit of Thy death."

This section of our study of the Wesleyan-Arminian emphasis on true holiness is concluded with the pertinent summary of an unidentified author:

"Entire sanctification makes us morally *pure* from our inbred depravity . . . the subject is *perfect* as to the kind of his Christianity or religion, yet not in such a way that the measure of it cannot be increased. He is *holy* in the sense that he is morally pure. He is *sinless* in the sense that his past sinful acts have all been pardoned and his corrupt nature cleansed. He is *blameless* in the sense that God sees in his pardoned and cleansed soul nothing condemned by the Gospel law. As to his *love* it is perfect in kind, and perfect in the sense that he loves with all the heart, mind, soul and strength; and in the sense that 'love is the fulfilling of the law,' and 'the bond of perfectness.' As to progress, he is growing in it. The measure, power, and intensity of his life is on continual increase. His soul made in kind heavenly, now matures in degree, and ripens for glorification. The imperfection that needs perfecting is the measure of that grace, not its kind."

CHAPTER NINE

John Wesley's Personal Experience of Christian Perfection

So intimately and correctly is John Wesley's name associated with the doctrine of Christian Perfection that it comes as a surprise to some to read the increasingly frequent assertions that Wesley never professed to have personally experienced what he taught as possible and necessary for others. The result of such assertions is that many feel that Wesley was inconsistent and that this may have been more of a theological abstraction or theory than a question of practical value.

One would be less surprised if these assertions came only from writers outside Methodism. But when one finds the denial that Wesley ever professed this as a personal experience being circulated by some in the highest offices in Methodism, it cannot be brushed aside as of no consequence. This matter deserves an accurate and exhaustive study of the words of those who make the denial and of Wesley himself. If it be true that Wesley did not profess the experience; or, what is of more value, that he did not possess it, those who assert that he did, should know the truth and desist from circulating erroneous claims for Wesley. If, on the other hand, it can be shown that he did possess and profess the experience, those who deny that he did should know the truth and desist from circulating further denials.

Unfortunately, the question as to Wesley's personal experience of Christian perfection is now answered by a simple "Yes" or "No." To ascertain the facts, it is necessary to make careful research and to document the material. It is not enough to say: "Wesley said ..." Neither are fragmentary quotations desirable, although an article of this nature allows only brief quotations from original sources. These will be cited in order that those who wish to refer to them may do so. Wesley complained to Bishop

Lavington that he (the bishop) had cited and murdered four or five lines from one of his Journals; and objected to his using "incoherent scraps (by which you make anything out of anything)" instead of using "entire connected sentences." Wesley argued that such a procedure misinterpreted and misrepresented his actual position.[1]

Some Undeniable Facts

Wesley's entire life was marked by a quest for holiness which he in his mature years taught as a doctrine to be believed, an experience to be received, and a life to be lived. Some of his statements on this doctrine appear confusing and at times contradictory unless one bears in mind that Wesley was more concerned with the life of holiness than with any theory about holiness;[2] and that he was "more interested in the experience than in its psychology"[3]; and that Wesley wrote for those in all stages of spiritual development from the awakened penitents who desired "to flee the wrath to come" to those maturing fathers in Christ. Thus one finds him speaking and writing, to various ones at different times, of this great experience as a present, instantaneous attainment (which he acknowledges some to have experienced), and at other times he writes and speaks of it to others as a future and (to them) as yet "unrealized ideal." Despite the fact that his teachings on Christian Perfection subjected him to abuses and calumnies by avowed enemies, and became the basis for unwarranted extremes by professed "friends" of his views, Wesley considered his teachings on the subject to be a vital part of his message on a free, full and felt salvation. It was discussed frequently in the "Conferences" and occupied a large place in his writings and sermons because he felt it to be a truth which God "peculiarly entrusted to the Methodists."[4] He also declared in a letter written in September, 1790, that this was "The grand depositum which God has lodged with the Methodists."[5] The preaching of Christian Perfection as a present possibility aroused hostility in Wesley's day, even as it does in our own day, because, as Dimond says, it "challenged both the moral standards and the current orthodoxy...."[6]

Nor can one dispute the fact that there is an increasing

number of writers who deny that Wesley ever professed to have personally experienced the Christian Perfection which he preached to, and required of, others. The first such author of which this writer is aware is L. Tyerman. His work appeared eighty years after Wesley's death. Bishop Edwin D. Mouzon, Dr. J. S. Simon, Dr. R. Newton Flew, Dr. Maximin Piette, Bishop Francis J. McConnell, Dr. W. E. Sangster, and Bishop John M. Moore with one voice agree that Wesley never professed to have personally experienced Christian Perfection. On the other hand, there is no disputing the fact that the writers who were personally acquainted with Wesley's terminology and profession not only do not deny his personally experiencing this great privilege and duty of the Christian life, they never intimate anything to raise a question about his having experienced it. We shall later consider statements made by some of Wesley's contemporaries; but in the meantime, it seems strange for Methodist authors to repeat what Tyerman suggested about Wesley's personal experience of Christian Perfection when some of them suggest that his words about Wesley's life at College are too strong. It reminds one of the adage that what a man had rather were true, he the more readily believes. The evidence is that the further Methodism gets from realizing that Christian Perfection is its "grand depositum," and the more unpopular its proclamation as a present, personal experience becomes, the more frequent are the denials that Wesley ever professed it as a personal experience. As long as Methodism put the emphasis on a free, full, felt salvation by faith, there was neither time nor place for such a denial. But when salvation by culture began to receive attention, there was no felt need for the second birth; and theologians who do not proclaim the second birth cannot be expected to promote "the second blessing, properly so called," as Wesley designated it.[7] History has vindicated Wesley's views that this doctrine was vital to Methodism's spiritual progress.

A Glimpse of Wesley's Day

A better understanding of Wesley and the question at issue will be possible if he is measured against the prevailing conditions in Eighteenth Century England. It is unfair to judge any man by conditions which prevailed two centuries before or after his day. Green deals with Wesley's day as "The Revolution." Chapters 9 and 10 afford a clear picture of conditions between 1660 and 1815.[8] A perusal of other sources, particularly Dr. J. S. Simon,[9] will show that despite the spiritual apathy of the most of the clergymen of that period, there was considerable religious activity. But that did not prevent its being a period of conflict and controversy in religion as well as in politics, for the two were intimately connected through the State Church. Thus it is no wonder that often Wesley and his cause were attacked at the same time by opposing groups, one of which called him a Papist and the other a Puritan; for each feared that the Methodist movement aimed at restoring the other to power.

The clergy in general was so fearful of offending some of the contenders in the controversies that an inoffensive, colorless, impractical and ineffective type of preaching became popular. In order to maintain "moderation" and avoid the charge of "enthusiasm," theology was allowed to lose its definiteness and its vivifying power, with the result that "preaching too much generated into the mere moral essay."[10] Many came to fear that the spiritual consciousness of the masses was beyond recovery. The outlook seemed almost hopeless, unless man endured as seeing the invisible.

Wesley's day was also characterized by extravagance as well as controversy. The religious controversy over "the most fundamental points" became as acute as the political controversy, with the result that "questions of directly practical import" were ignored. England faced the sad fact that "the doctrine (of Christianity) was accepted, but the life was not lived."[11] To those who were thus so nearly morally and spiritually deadened, "the grand controversy was who could outeat, outdrink and outdress his neighbor." It is no surprise that in such an age, Wesley's pure and practical teachings, coupled with his exemplary piety and noble aspirations, evoked opposition. Where he hoped to find sympathy with his religious ideals, he too often found unbelief and criticism. His display of kindness and charity was rewarded with barbarous and vulgar abuse.

His simplicity in speech was scorned by those who wanted the elaborate, ornate, and vehement in oratory which made them appear to possess great learning. Wesley carefully avoided all "nice and philosophical speculations" and "perplexed and intricate reasonings," as well as "those kinds of technical terms that so frequently occur in Bodies of Divinity."

The frankness with which Wesley reproved any professor of religion for his inconsistencies provoked bitter persecution. He knew "Oxford University ... to be the residence of rakes and idlers and debauchees." It was not uncommon for clergymen to be so intoxicated, even when expounding the Bible, as to require assistance from others lest they fall. One Oxford lad wrote his mother that he had seen his tutor "carried off perfectly intoxicated." And it is said that one Oxford professor "died after drinking late at his own house with the Vice-Chancellor (who is the actual head of the University) and some others."[12]

Dr. George Peck says that Wesley was called a Papist, a Ranter, a Pelagian, an enthusiast, and a heretic. He also quotes the Works of Augustus Toplady, wherein Toplady declares: "The supposition of possible perfection on earth is the most fanatic dream, and the most gigantic delusion which can whirl the brain of a human being."[13] A more complete view of the various extremes and extravagances of his age can be gleaned from Dr. J. H. Whiteley who gave life-size, natural-color pictures of the "artificial society" which Wesley attacked, and which in turn attacked Wesley.[14]

As an aid to a clearer understanding of what may be involved in the question at issue—Did Wesley personally profess to have experienced Christian Perfection?—it will be well to bear in mind Whiteley's words about eighteenth-century language; for it is with words that we have to do in considering this question. Said he: "This artificial society was also fond of hounding to death for a brief time some inoffensive word, utterly regardless of the word's derivative or accidental meaning. . . . As with other centuries, the eighteenth had its full share in the change of the meaning in words themselves, and many everyday words became elevated or degraded in significance and narrowed or widened in meaning through the course of these hundred years.... Wesley's hymns, letters, and diaries also exemplify this perpetual change in word meanings...."[15]

The Basis of the Contention

Before quoting Wesley, it seems best to consider the contention of those who deny that he professed Christian Perfection as a personal experience. The first assertion will be that of Dr. L. Tyerman who, after quoting Wesley's letter to Lloyd's Evening Post (London) on April 3, 1767, in which he answered attacks repeatedly made on him in the Christian Magazine, says: "The above is an important letter, were it for nothing else than showing that Wesley preached a doctrine he himself did not experience. For above thirty years, he had taught the doctrine of Christian Perfection; but here he flatly declares, that, as yet he had not attained to it: he taught it, not because he felt it, but because he believed the Bible taught it."[16]

In The Standard Sermons of John Wesley, annotated by Dr. E. H. Sugden, is this comment in his introduction to Wesley's Sermon XXXV on Christian Perfection:

"He [Wesley] never professed himself to have received it. Logically, he could see no reason why the ideal could not be at any time realized, provided a man had the requisite faith; but he came more and more to see that it was an ideal to which the believer approximates ever more closely, though it may be impossible to say that he has absolutely attained it."[17]

Bishop Edwin D. Mouzon wrote: "In the genesis and growth of Methodism, the true order is: First, experience and a holy life, and then Christian doctrine. Doctrine grows out of experience and life."[18] Elsewhere he declared:

"It is interesting to know that Wesley did not himself profess it (Christian Perfection). To one who had objected to the doctrine, Mr. Wesley wrote: 'I tell you flat, I have not attained the character I draw.' The nearest he is known to have come to professing it was to the question whether he had ever experienced the blessing of perfect love, he replied by quoting Charles Wesley's hymn: 'Jesus, confirm my heart's desire....' "[19]

Thus it is seen that Bishop Mouzon refers to the letter

Tyerman quoted, and since that letter is apparently the basis for the denial that Wesley professed to have personally experienced Christian Perfection, the letter will be given special attention in a subsequent section of this study.

Dr. J. S. Simon says: "It is well known that he (Wesley) never made claim to have reached 'perfection,' but he never lost sight of the goal. He pressed forward, longing to attain approval of his sympathizing Judge."[20]

Dr. R. Newton Flew, who writes in a sympathetic vein, seems more inclined to raise a question than to assert a denial; although in mentioning Thomas Walsh, "Wesley's typical helper," he says: "It is notable that he, like Wesley himself, never claimed to have attained the goal."[21] After conceding that Dr. Curtis's theory that he had found the exact time when Wesley professed to have experienced Christian Perfection could not be proved or disproved and that the passage Curtis cites was "one indication among others that he himself (Wesley) had entered into the supernatural realm of conquest and abiding peace . . . ," Flew commented: "But the difficulty still remains. How did it come to pass that the apostle of the Evangelical Revival . . . himself never bore such a testimony? Was it some fastidiousness, some half-unconscious suspicion that avowal would be perilous to the health of his soul?"[22]

Father Piette, the Catholic writer whose research on Wesley was vast when treating "The Wesleyan Doctrine," asks: "And what of perfection? Can absolute perfection be attained in this world? Wesley at times had said so; and some of his followers have, here and there, claimed to be in this state of perfect sanctity . . . but Wesley had the good sense never to believe that he had attained to the heights of sanctity—a fact which, seeing the life he lived, says much for his deep-seated humility."[23]

But Wesley's Sermon on Christian Perfection[24] refutes the suggestion that he taught that absolute perfection was attainable in this life.

In one of his earlier books, Bishop Francis J. McConnell wrote: "Careful students of John Wesley's life have insisted that he never claimed the blessing of entire sanctification for himself."[25] But in his biography of John Wesley, the bishop declared:

"It will be recalled that Wesley never claimed himself to have reached what he called 'Christian perfection.' Psychologists and theologians have perused the Journal line by line to find some single statement on which they could themselves base a claim for such an experience for him. Some have fancied that they have found not a claim, but a proof in a passage here or there...."[26]

A comparatively recent author, whose book has been widely read and discussed, suggests:

"It will be felt by many that Wesley was inconsistent in making this doctrine [Christian Perfection] central in his teaching, urging his people to 'press on to perfection,' and to testify concerning it, yet never testifying himself . . . but whatever testifying he urged upon his people, he never said himself, 'I am freed from sin. . . .' "[27]

One other denial will be considered sufficient. This one is from the pen of Bishop John M. Moore:

"Mr. Wesley believed in the doctrine of Christian perfection, perfect love, holiness, and entire sanctification but he never claimed for himself the experience . . . he never gave any date for a second experience that brought Christian perfection or entire sanctification. . . . He was far from being dogmatic in his opinion as to when and how sanctification came. That could not have been so with him had he been convinced by any Scripture text as to the time and manner of the experience."[28]

Only two of those who issued denials that Wesley ever professed to have experienced Christian Perfection cited any authority for their denials: Tyerman and Bishop Mouzon; and both of them cited the same document. But these two disagree on other points, for Tyerman asserts that Wesley taught Christian perfection "not because he felt it"—evidently meaning that he did not experience it—"but because he believed the Bible taught it." Bishop Mouzon compared the genesis and growth of Methodism to history covered by the New Testament, and declared: "The true order is: First, experience and a holy life, and then Christian doctrine. Doctrine grows out of experience and life."

Apropos of the relation of doctrine to experience and life, Dr. Samuel Chadwick, a renowned English Methodist author, who also served as a college principal, a president of the Methodist Conference, a president of the Southport Convention, and editor of a religious publication, wrote:

"Methodism was born of God in the warm heart of its founder.... Wesley preached Christ as he realized Him in his own soul. The Methodist doctrines of conversion, assurance, and full salvation can be traced to marked crises in his own experience of the saving grace of God. The Methodist peculiarities of fellowship, testimony, and aggression were all first exemplified in the religious life of the first Methodist."[29]

Both Dr. Sugden and Father Piette used words that Wesley shunned to relate to personal experience. They used the terms "absolutely attained" and "absolute perfection." Knowing man's frailty, Wesley avoided any term which might suggest that man could reach a state on earth where improvement was not possible or desirable. And in his *Plain Account of Christian Perfection,*[30] Wesley declares that to have infallible proof that one has attained the experience he might profess, it would be necessary for God to endow him "with the miraculous discernment of spirits." And Wesley was so fearful that the Methodists would rest in an attained "state" that he avoided using that term, for he believed and taught that beyond the crisis of cleansing of the heart, there was a necessary progressive development of the sanctified life.

Dr. Flew's query as to why Wesley did not give clear testimony to his personal experience will be treated in a subsequent section. But Dr. Sangster's denial and contention, based on Wesley's not using a specific pattern moulded for him by another century and a half after his death, seems unreasonable—and doubly so when one knows the variety of terms Wesley used in describing this experience. He believed in the destruction of sin, and contended for it, according to his Letters.[31] In his correspondence with Joseph Benson, Wesley declares that he used the word "destroyed" because St. Paul used it, and he did not find the word "suspended" in the Bible. In a letter to Benson, dated December 28, 1770, Wesley says:

"And you allow the whole thing which I contend for—an entire deliverance from sin, a recovery of the whole image of God, the loving God with all our heart, soul, and strength. And you believe God is able to give you this—yea, to give it to you in an instant. You trust He will."

But as to using anything which suggested "sinless perfection" Wesley avoided all such references. He knew what use his enemies and the misguided and uninformed would make of such an expression. "Sinless perfection is a phrase I never use lest I should seem to contradict myself." "Is, then, the term, sinless perfection, proper? It is not worth disputing about."[32]

Dr. Sangster's objection begins to lose much of its weight when one considers the varied terminology Wesley used in connection with this experience. He spoke of it as "perfect love," "glorious liberty," "full salvation," "the whole image of God," "pure love of God," "the second change," "the second blessing," "renewed in love," "full sanctification," "holiness," "a clean heart," "entire sanctification," "Christian perfection," "perfected in love," "saved from sin," "entire deliverance from sin," "the root of sin taken away," "full redemption," "full renewal in His image," "sanctification," "cleansing from all sin," "renewed in love," "full liberty," etc.[33]

Bishop McConnell, in his book, *John Wesley*, suggests that the denial that Wesley professed Christian Perfection as a personal experience presents a "strange situation" since for a half century Wesley preached it as "the heart of Methodist belief and practice." The bishop then raises two questions: (1) Whether Wesley's followers "assumed" that his personal experience was up to the standard he urged upon them; or, (2) whether they were willing to let Wesley be what he wanted to be and to say what he wanted to say, without bothering to ask questions. Since there is preserved a sufficient quantity of the correspondence which passed between Wesley and his colleagues, and many others, no prolonged consideration need be given the question as to whether questions were asked about his personal experience. We know there were. He was severely criticized by some of his enemies who did not know whereof they spoke, and who were incensed because Wesley did not, for reasons he deemed sufficient to himself, tell them all he knew.[34] The Select Societies afforded ample opportunity for close questioning by each member concerning the personal experience of the others present. Many of the questions asked and the replies given were both forthright and unadorned. They were soul-searching. The other question as to whether his followers assumed that Wesley's experience was up to "the type" he set for them will be considered in a subsequent section of this study.

Wesley Speaks for Himself

As one studies the quotations from Wesley's own writings, he will have a better understanding of his meaning and will be aided in arriving at a clearer conception of Wesley's position if he will bear in mind, as Piette mentions, that the years prior to 1741 were Wesley's "formation years." In them, he was shaping his views and maturing them. Wesley seems to have been always "fascinated" by the practical side of religion and he seems not to have had time for "flights of speculative imagination." At times, one will question whether or not there is any coherence between some of his writings, but if it be borne in mind that all Wesley's writings are characterized by an appeal to personal religious experience, he will be found to be consistent and coherent. Piette felt that:

"Since practical experience and experimentation had been triumphant in the field of natural science, Wesley was led to transport it to the religious domain—to the field of the supernatural life. Around his own personal experiences, and those he was familiar with in his disciples, he gathered and polarized all his theological writings."[35]

It will also greatly assist one in understanding Wesley's writings to remember what an incessant traveler and preacher he was, in addition to his task of preparing voluminous publications for the press, much of which was done while riding or being entertained away from access to his reference books, etc. If at different times he may be found to express himself in different ways, it may be far more correct to consider that his later writings were "corrections" of his former views than contradictions of them.

Bishop Neely says: "Where we can find what he meant

to be an exact use or definition, then the other uses should be explained by, and harmonized with, that, and not the exact use by the others. The precise and clear statement is to be used to interpret the uncertain, and not the reverse." And he concludes his chapter on "Interpreting Wesley" by saying: "When one undertakes to interpret John Wesley, he should take first, his specific statements, when he seeks to be exact; and, second, his maturest expressions."[36]

In Wesley's earlier days, he had "an exceeding complex idea of sanctification, or a sanctified man."[37] On January 1, 1733, he preached a sermon before Oxford University on "The Circumcision of the Heart" which became the first of his published writings; and in that sermon, Wesley said:

"It is that habitual disposition of soul which, in the sacred writings, is termed holiness; and which directly implies the being cleansed 'from all filthiness of flesh and spirit'; and by consequence, the being endued with those virtues which were in Christ Jesus; the being so 'renewed in the image of our mind' as to be 'perfect as our Father in heaven is perfect.'"

In the same sermon, he also said: "Love is the fulfilling of the law, the end of the commandment. It is not only 'the first and great command, but all the commandments in one....'" And in 1777, he declared that this was the "view of religion I then had, which even then I scrupled not to call perfection. This is the view I have of it now, without any material addition or diminution."[38]

In the Preface to the second editon of Hymns (1742) Wesley, recognizing that the dispute over Christian Perfection was now "at the height" and seeking to dispel as much as possible of the "general prejudice" which had arisen from "a misapprehension of the nature of it," set forth, as clearly as words afford, a practical description of what he meant by "one that is perfect." Such a person was one in whom is "the mind of Christ," and who so "walketh as Christ also walked"; a man that "hath clean hands and a pure heart," or that is "cleansed from all filthiness of flesh and spirit" ... and one who, accordingly, "does not commit sin" ... one whom God hath "sanctified throughout in body, soul, and spirit" ... one who "walketh in the light as

He is in the light, in whom is no darkness at all; the blood of Jesus Christ His Son having cleansed him from all sin".... In other words, to be inwardly and outwardly devoted to God; all devoted in heart and life.[39]

The Conference Minutes of 1759 contain this record:

Q. What is Christian Perfection? A. 1. The loving God with all our heart, mind, soul, and strength; and our neighbor as ourselves, which implies deliverance from all sin; 2. That this is received by faith; 3. That it is given instantaneously, in one moment; 4. That we are to expect it (not at death) but every moment; 5. That now is the accepted time, now is the day of salvation.[40]

In Wesley's examination of those who professed to be sanctified, he was exceedingly careful to ask not only whether they committed outward sins, but to ask whether they felt any inward sin. His Journal for March 12, 1760, reports that he spent the greater part of the day "examining . . . one by one" many who professed to believe that they were saved from sin. He was convinced (1) that they feel no inward sin, and to the best of their knowledge commit no outward sin; (2) that they see and love God every moment, and pray, rejoice, give thanks evermore; (3) that they have constantly as clear witness from God of sanctification as they have of justification. "Now in this I do rejoice, and will rejoice, call it what you please; and I would to God that thousands had experienced thus much, let them afterward experience as much more as God pleases." Thus while he did not contend over the name by which the experience was called, he was careful to see that those who professed to have the experience manifested the life that proved Christian perfection to be practical as well as theoretical. His words about experiencing as much as God pleases show that he did not consider this a finality, but a fitness for service.

In 1767, Wesley wrote: "By perfection I mean the humble, gentle, patient love of God and our neighbor, ruling our tempers, words, and actions. . . . I do not contend for the term sinless, though I do not object against it...." One has said that Wesley was not dogmatic about the time and manner of receiving the experience, but he does speak clearly and positively about "the manner and time of receiving it" in his writings.

"As to the manner, I believe this perfection is always wrought in the soul by a simple act of faith; consequently, in an instant. As to the time: I believe this instant is generally the instant of death. . . . But I believe it may be ten, twenty, or forty years before. I believe it is usually many years after justification; but that it may be within five years or five months after it, I know no conclusive argument to the contrary. If it must be many years after justification, I would be glad to know how many. . . ."[41]

Wesley, with his realistic view of life, admitted that there usually was a delay between the two experiences, because sometimes there were those who needed to be instructed as to the nature and conditions of the experience. But such a delay was not necessary. The great theological controversies of the day often raged about the words "necessary" and "necessity" and so Wesley demands proof that a long delay is necessary.

His letter to his brother Charles, dated June 27, 1766, shows how urgent John Wesley was to have the instantaneousness of this blessing pressed. "O insist everywhere on full redemption, receivable by faith alone! Consequently to be looked for now. You are made, as it were, for this very thing. Just here you are in your element. In connection I beat you; but in strong, pointed sentences you beat me. Go on, in your own way, in what God has peculiarly called you to do. Press the instantaneous blessing; then I shall have more time for my peculiar calling, enforcing the gradual work."[42]

At the Conference of 1768, following several years of disappointments and controversies and apparent decline of the work, the question arose as to how God's work might be revived and enlarged. One suggestion was: Preach Christian Perfection! It was to be preached "as a gradual and instantaneous blessing" with believers reminded that it was their privilege. Thereupon, Mr. Wesley said:

"That we all may speak the same thing, I ask, once for all, shall we defend this Perfection, or give it up? You all agree to defend it, meaning thereby, as we did from the beginning, Salvation from all sin by the love of God and our neighbor filling the heart. . . . You are all agreed, we may be saved from all sin before death. The substance then is settled. But as to the circumstance: Is the change instantaneous or gradual? It is both the one and other. From the moment we are justified, there may be a gradual sanctification, or a growing in grace, a daily advance in the knowledge and love of God. And if sin cease before death, there must in the nature of the things be an instantaneous change. There must be a last moment when it does exist and first moment wherein it does not. . . ."[43]

The conclusion of the matter was: Whoever would advance the gradual change in believers should strongly insist upon the instantaneous because when the hope of an instantaneous deliverance from sin is destroyed, "salvation stands still, or rather decreases daily."

Lest someone say that this desire to press the instantaneous blessing waned as Wesley grew older, consider his letter to Sarah Rutter, dated December 5, 1789 (sixteen months before his death): "Full deliverance from sin, I believe, is always instantaneous—at least, I never yet knew an exception. . . ."[44]

In his sermon on *The Scriptural Way of Salvation*, Wesley defines "salvation" as including "the entire work of God, from the first dawning of grace in the soul, till it is consummated in glory." That agrees with Wesley's views that sanctification begins in regeneration, is made full or entire in the second crisis or experience which he designated "the second blessing" or "the second change" as he may choose, and is subsequently perfected and developed by growth in grace and in the knowledge and love of God.[45] "This [salvation] consists of two general parts, justification and sanctification. Justification is another word for pardon."[46] And in the state of pardon, with sanctification begun, "we wait for entire sanctification; for a full salvation from all our sins—from pride, self-will, anger, unbelief; or as the Apostle expresses it, 'go on unto perfection.' But what is perfection? The word has various senses; here it means perfect love. It is love excluding sin; love filling the heart, taking up the whole capacity of the soul. . . ."[47]

Bishop Mouzon quotes Wesley thus: "I mean loving

God with all our heart and our neighbor as ourselves. I pin all its opponents to this definition. No evasion. No shifting the question." In his words to those who cavil about professors of holiness not meeting their expectation, because, as Wesley told them, they included more in their demands of such "perfect" Christians than the Scriptures warranted, he said: "Pure love reigning alone in the heart and life—this is the whole of scriptural perfection."[48] It will be well to remember the words of this paragraph when considering the alleged denial of perfection as a personal experience by John Wesley.

As to the condition for receiving sanctification, Wesley declared that it is received by faith.

"Faith is the condition, and the only condition, of sanctification, exactly as it is of justification. It is the condition: no one is sanctified but he that believes; without faith no man is sanctified. And it is the only condition: this alone is sufficient for sanctification. Every one that believes is sanctified, whatever else he has or has not. In other words, no man is sanctified till he believes: every man when he believes is sanctified. . . . But what is that faith whereby we are sanctified—saved from sin, and perfected in love? It is a divine evidence and conviction, first, that God hath promised it in the holy Scriptures . . . secondly, that what God hath promised He is able to perform . . . thirdly, that He is able and willing to do it now. And why not? . . . To this confidence, that God is both able and willing to sanctify us now, there needs to be added one thing more—a divine evidence and conviction that He doeth it. In that hour, it is done. . . ."[49]

Faith, scriptural faith, meant to Wesley that "attitude of the human mind by which it realizes the invisible, the imponderable and intangible, and actualizes them in time and space for divine purposes. It cooperates with the will of God."[50] Thus to John Wesley, if one had true faith in the power, promises, and purposes of God, there was nothing unreasonable in the believer's praying for Christian perfection and expecting God to give it to him when he prayed and believed for it, thus granting him his prayer for deliverance from sin and the assurance of the Spirit.

The Cause of the Contention

Two sentences in a letter that John Wesley wrote seem to be the basis of the insistent denial that he ever professed to have experienced perfect love, or entire sanctification. That letter to the Editor of *Lloyd's Evening Post* (London), dated March 5, 1767, was published on April 3, 1767. An explanation of its origin and contents is in order: In 1756 a popular young clergyman of London, afterward the famous Dr. Dodd, questioned Wesley on his views concerning Christian Perfection, and Wesley, then twice the young man's age, courteously replied. The young man was admittedly one of London's most popular young ministers, able but extravagant and vain. To augment his income he wrote for the religious press, and the *Christian Magazine* gave him one hundred pounds per year for his services. At length, after Dodd, using an assumed name, had misrepresented Wesley's views and had unjustly misrepresented the Methodists and their cause, Wesley reluctantly made a public reply.[51] Seven years after this letter was published, Dodd's effort to secure a lucrative appointment by bribery exposed him to public scorn and he retired to France, where he lived for three years. Returning to England in 1777, he forged a draft for a large sum. He was convicted and sentenced to be hanged, and despite a great appeal in his behalf, he was hanged as a felon. But between his arrest and his execution, he sought help from Wesley and the Methodists whom he had misrepresented and abused, and they kindly ministered to him until his execution. In this they returned good for evil, as they preached.

In his correspondence of March 12, 1756, Wesley declared to Dodd that by his teaching on Christian Perfection, "I never meant any more by perfection than loving God with all our heart and serving Him with all our strength. But I dare not say less than this. . . ." Wesley also made it plain to him that in his view of perfection, there was the possibility and need for continual development in the life of one who had been made perfect in love. But it was Dodd's misrepresentation of statements in Wesley's article entitled *The Character of a Methodist* that caused Wesley "to enter the lists with him." Dodd had said: "A Methodist, according to Mr. Wesley, is one who is perfect, and sinneth not in thought, word, or deed." That was making Wesley say words he never used and did not intend to use. Wesley was careful with his words and wanted each one used as he intended it, and as he interpreted it. Repeatedly in his controversies, he showed the unfairness of adding, omitting, or otherwise misusing even one word. Thus, this exact man in the midst of careless men would not allow a wilful misrepresentation of his supposedly direct words to go unreproved. He knew that Dodd held erroneous views on perfection, and that he sought every possible opportunity to misrepresent the Methodist, whom he accused of intending a secession from the Church. Desirous of defending the truth and of rebuking such flagrant abuse of one's words, Wesley sent a letter to the public press in which appear these sentences: "I have told all the world, I am not perfect; and yet you allow me to be a Methodist. I tell you flat, I have not attained the character I draw...." Then Wesley passes to deny the charge that "Other Methodists have" attained perfection in the sense Dodd had intended to claim for them. His words are "I say no such thing." He thereupon declared that after setting forth a scriptural portrait of a perfect Christian, he had written: "By these marks the Methodists desire to be distinguished from other men; by these we labour to distinguish ourselves." In this letter, Wesley does not deny Christian perfection as a personal possession any more than he denies that any Methodist possessed it. He denied being perfect in the incorrect, unscriptural and unreasonable sense that Dodd and his school of thinkers would have liked to have fastened upon them; but the seeker after truth must consider the words in their setting and not isolate them from their context and from the situations facing Wesley in this controversy.

In this connection, Wesley knew that those who enjoyed the highest possible state of grace attainable on earth must dwell in shattered bodies and were thereby so pressed down at times that they could not always exert themselves as they would by speaking, thinking, and acting precisely right. He was consistent, therefore in denying that he or his followers professed to be "perfect" in the sense their detractors charged. Wesley had written:

"For want of better bodily organs, they must at times think, speak, or act wrongly; not indeed through a defect of love, but through a defect of knowledge; and while this is the case, notwithstanding that defect, and its consequences, they fulfill the law of love."[52]

But to get the full sense of Wesley's meaning in these two sentences, and to appreciate the purpose of the whole letter in question, one ought to read the last lines of this "important" letter. Wesley's attackers consider the profession of "perfection" to involve practically a renunciation of one's dependence upon the mercy of God and the merits of the Saviour. Wesley's denial of that kind of perfection for himself and the Methodists was laudable, not blameable. He was thinking of their going to the table of the Lord for communion, and by his denial of any professed experience that trusted in self instead of the Saviour, he was removing them from the suspicion of insincerity when they went to the table of the Lord. Thus a great deal more was at issue in the letter Wesley wrote than whether or not he personally professed a certain experience which he taught as desirable and possible, as well as scriptural.

Concerning this letter and the use Wesley's critics have made of it, it will be well to bear in mind that Wesley lived twenty-four years after it was published. Insofar as can be ascertained, he was never called in question by a colleague or the Conference over it, nor did he deem it needful to offer any explanation for it in his writings. None of his contemporaries who wrote an account of his life and times felt it needful to mention, explain, or otherwise account for the statement. Insofar as is known to this writer, Tyerman, who published his works more than a century after the letter appeared in print, is the first to use it as a proof that Wesley disclaimed Christian Perfection as a personal experience. It is apparent that Wesley, his contemporaries and his critics understood what he meant in this letter and were satisfied with his explanation.

One of the bishops, quoted as affirming that Wesley did not profess the personal experience of Christian perfection, bases his position on Wesley's not saying so in the exact words of a forthright claim. But the bishop took the position that one's profession to be perfect would be positive proof that he was not perfect. By that line of reasoning, one might expect him to concede that Wesley possessed the experience but modestly refrained from professing it lest he be accused of boasting. Instead, he feels that he did not have it, or he would have professed it; although his reasoning would be that if he had professed it, that would have proved he did not have it.

Did Wesley Profess Christian Perfection?

It is believed that there is evidence enough to satisfy any unprejudiced person that Wesley did profess Christian Perfection. Since it was his correspondence with Dodd that evoked the letter, which has been cited to deny Wesley's profession of Christian Perfection, consistency would lead one to study their correspondence on the subject of Perfection. On March 12, 1756, Wesley wrote Dodd and mentioned his sermon on *Salvation By Faith* and dealt with Dodd's use of his words about the believer's freedom from sin. Then comes this comment: "I must still aver they (the Scripture used) speak both my own experience and that of many hundred children of God whom I personally know."[53]

Wesley's personal experience was criticized by some who claimed that by their discernment he was not living as close to God as he should. Candidly Wesley asked who knew whether he lived more or less closely with God, and attributed such accusations to their "surmisings" with which God was not pleased. He acknowledged in this letter that it was hard for him to speak of himself, but he said: "You know something of my own testimony." Thus Wesley indicated that he did speak more freely to some than to others about his personal experience and relationship to God. In this connection, there are other words which are highly important in this study of his personal experience. He said that if his critics would observe his "outward walking"—which was the acid test of a profession, in Wesley's estimate—he was "bold to say" that they would "see nothing but what might become Gregory Lopez."[54]

The mention of Lopez arrests our attention. No student of Wesley's personal experience of perfection seems to have given this reference serious thought. Lopez was a Spanish missionary to the West Indies, and Wesley read and reread his life, carrying a long account of his life and labors in the *Arminian Magazine* in 1780 and including a life of Lopez in his *Christian Library*. Wesley's words in connection with Lopez are:

"For years, I despaired of finding any inhabitant of Great Britain that could stand in any degree of comparison with Gregory Lopez or M. DeRenty. But let any impartial person judge if Mr. Fletcher was at all inferior to them."[55]

By thus connecting and comparing his own "outward walking" with Lopez, and by connecting Lopez with the sainted Fletcher, Wesley is modestly and truthfully testifying to his own attainments in the grace of God. Lopez further influenced Wesley in his reticence about speaking all he knew. Wesley vindicated his own silence, when words would have satisfied many, by saying: "I answer with him (Lopez), 'I do not speak all I know, but what I judge needful.' "[56] Thus, there was a reason for his speech.

In the *Plain Account of Christian Perfection*, the question is asked: "How may we certainly know one that is saved from all sin?" And after an explanation as to the difference between knowing "infallibly," which would involve the possession of the divine gift of discernment of spirits, comes the answer:

"We would deem these to be sufficient proofs to any reasonable man, and such as would leave little room to doubt either the truth or depth of the work: (1) If we had clear evidence of his exemplary behavior for some time before this supposed change. This would give us reason to believe he would not 'lie for God,' but speak neither more nor less than he felt; (2) If he gave a distinct account of the time and manner wherein the change was wrought, which sound speech could not be reproved; and (3) If it appeared that all his subsequent words and actions were holy and unblameable."[57]

In reading the *Plain Account*, one detects a decided change of tone in some of the questions which, in view of the different views of some members of the "Conference" out of which these questions and answers grew, is of importance. At some points, Wesley generalizes with such expressions as "we," "you," "he," etc. But when he cites his own views, he uses the first person, "I." A case in point: They were discussing how to distinguish between "temptation" and "corruption of the heart." There Wesley uses the personal pronoun, "I." "I feel no pride"; "I feel no anger at all"; "I feel no desire or lust at all"; and he continues by saying: "The difference is still plainer when I compare my present state with my past, wherein I felt temptation and corruption, too." This personal testimony is followed at once by a specific question: "How do you know that you are sanctified—saved from your inbred corruption?" The answer comes equally direct:

"I can know no otherwise than I know I am justified. 'Hereby know we that we are of God (in either case), by the Spirit He hath given us.' We know it by the witness and fruit of the Spirit. . . ."

And in this same paragraph, Wesley uses the expression: "When we are sanctified, He (the Spirit) bore witness that they (our sins) were taken away" as distinguished from "forgiven" "when we are justified."[58]

One of the authorities cited as denying Wesley's personal profession of Christian Perfection complained that Wesley did not bear "testimony." Let him ponder these words: "I have continually testified in private and in public, that we are sanctified as well as justified by faith."[59] If Wesley's words mean anything, the following quotation from a letter to Lady Huntington, dated June 19, 1771, sheds light on the question:

"Many years since, I saw that 'without holiness no man shall see the Lord.' I began following after it and inciting all with whom I had any intercourse to do the same. Ten years after, God gave me a clearer view than I had before of the way to attain this—namely, by faith in the Son of God. And immediately I declared to all, 'We are saved from sin, we are made holy, by faith.' This I testified in private, in public, in print; and God confirmed it by a thousand witnesses. I have continued to declare this for above thirty years, and God hath continued to confirm the word of His grace."[60]

This item is recorded in the Journal for October 28, 1762: "Many years ago my brother frequently said, 'Your day of Pentecost is not fully come; but I doubt not it will; and you will then hear of persons sanctified as frequently as you do now of persons justified.' Any unprejudiced reader may observe that it was now fully come."[61]

A fuller description of this is given elsewhere. "Any unprejudiced person who has read the accounts in my Journals may observe, that it was now fully come."[62] And this author observed that Wesley "frequently noted the work at this time, as being what St. Paul calls, The Perfecting of the Saints."

During the Bell-Maxfield controversy, on November 2, 1762, Wesley wrote Thomas Maxfield and commented with his usual candor ("and he never failed in candor," according to Flew) upon what he liked and disliked in teachings and conduct of Maxfield, Bell and their associates:

"I like your doctrine of Perfection, or pure love; love excluding sin; your insisting that it is merely by faith; that consequently, it is instantaneous (though preceded and followed by a gradual work), and that it may be now, at this instant. . . . I dislike the saying, This is not known nor taught among us till within two or three years. I grant you did not know it. You have over and over denied instantaneous sanctification to me; but I have known and taught it (and so has my brother, as our writings show) above these twenty years."[63]

Many believe that the moment Wesley experienced Christian Perfection is recorded in his Journal for December 24, 25, 1744.

"In the evening, while I was reading prayers at Snowsfield, I found such light and strength as I never remember to have had before, I saw every thought, as well as action or word, just as it was rising in my heart; and whether it was right before God or tainted with pride or selfishness. I never knew before (I mean not as at that time) what it was to 'be still before God.' I waked by the grace of God in the same spirit; and about eight, being with two or three that believed in Jesus, I felt such an awe and tender sense of the presence of God as greatly confirmed me therein: so that God was before me all the day long. I sought and found Him in every place; and could truly say, when I lay down at night, 'Now, I have lived a day.' "[64]

That testimony, measured by the tests to which Wesley subjected the professors of Christian Perfection, according to his Journal for March 12, 1760, bears striking resemblance in many respects. Dr. Olin A. Curtis comments thus on the Journal entry for December 24, 25, 1744:

"To any one familiar with John Wesley's careful, realistic manner of speech it is evident that we have here the same sort of testimony to the experience of holiness that we have in his Journal, May 24, 1738, to the experience of conversion. If the one is not quite so near a full definition as the others, it surely is just as expressive of the fact. I find it almost impossible to read Wesley's words in the light of all his later utterances about the doctrine of Christian perfection, and not consider this date, December 24, 1744, as the probable time when he began to love God supremely."[65]

This date agrees in general with the dates occasionally mentioned by Wesley in connection with the doctrine of Christian Perfection as it was understood and set forth by him and his brother. Unfortunately, Wesley's dates were not always as specific as one might wish on some points, but this is nothing against the fact of his experiencing this great grace. Dr. Mae A. Tenney of Greenville College (Illinois), a careful researcher on Wesley, wrote:

"Wesley does very little direct witnessing in his sermons and articles and Journal. Only once, he wrote of his heart-warming. And note, moreover, that he does not in that instance employ theological phraseology. One feels that Wesley avoided conventional, rubber-stamp terms."[66]

The value of the hymns as testimonies cannot be overlooked. When John Wesley went to use one of Dr. Henry More's hymns on *"The Descent of the Holy Ghost on the Day of Pentecost"* in the 1739 edition of *Hymns and Sacred Poems,* he changed the phraseology of this godly and contemplative man so that his words dealt with a personal and present blessing, instead of a wistful hope. The words were:

> Grant this, O holy God and true,
> Who the ancient prophets did inspire;
> Haste to perform Thy promise due,
> As all Thy servants Thee desire.

But Wesley altered the last two lines to read:

> To us perform the promise due;
> Descend and crown us now with fire.[67]

Consider also, in connection with Wesley's personal profession, that grand old hymn that he and the early Methodists sang, which closed with these words:

> Saviour, to Thee my soul looks up;
> My present Saviour Thou:
> In all the confidence of hope,
> I claim the blessing now.
> 'Tis done: Thou dost this moment save,
> With full salvation bless;
> Redemption through Thy blood I have
> And spotless love and peace.

And so we conclude: despite Wesley's reticence in speaking of his personal religious experience, lest he be accused of being a theological innovator or attract attention to himself and thereby detract attention from the gospel truths he wished men to accept; and lest he be accused of boasting and thereby injure the cause of Christ; and lest his testimony intensify the persecution of the members of the Methodist societies, we believe he did meekly, clearly and sufficiently witness to Christian Perfection as a personal experience and that his testimony leaves "no room for doubt that he professed to have the experience, and that he preached the doctrine of Christian Perfection and exhorted and encouraged his followers to seek it."[68]

Notes To Chapter One

[1] See article by Lauriston DuBois in *The Second Work of Grace*, D. Shelby Corlett, ed. (Kansas City, Mo.: Beacon Hill Press, n.d.), p. 142.

[2] G. A. McLaughlin, *Common Sense in Religion, or Reasons Why We Should Be Holy* (Chicago: Christian Witness Co., 1920), p. 1.

[3] "Article 9, Doctrines," *Pilgrim Church Manual*, 1958 edition (Indianapolis: Pilgrim Holiness Press).

[4] *Wesleyan Methodist Discipline* (Syracuse, N.Y.: Wesleyan Methodist Publishing Ass'n, 1959), p. 17.

[5] *Ibid.*, p. 23.

[6] R. A. Torrey, *Difficulties in the Bible* (Chicago: Moody Press, 1907), pp. 9-23.

[7] John Knox, *The Ethic of Jesus in the Teaching of the Church* (Nashville: Abingdon Press, 1962), p. 7.

[8] *Ibid.*, p. 97.

[9] Kenneth Scott Latourette, *A History of Christianity* (New York: Harper and Brothers, 1933), p. 786.

Notes To Chapter Two

[1] Randolph S. Foster, *The Philosophy of Christian Experience* (New York: Hunt and Eaton, 1891), pp. 159, 160.

[2] *Ibid.*, p. 10.

[3] James B. Chapman, *Holiness Triumphant* (Kansas City, Mo.: Beacon Hill Press, 1949), pp. 15, 16.

[4] Peter Wiseman's quote in pamphlet, *Definitions of Christian Doctrines.*

[5] John Wesley.

[6] Adam Clarke, *Christian Theology* (New York: Lane and Scott, 1849), p. 182.

[7] *Ibid.*, p. 199.

[8] J. G. Morrison, *Our Lost Estate* (Kansas City, Mo.: Nazarene Publishing House, 1929), p. 94.

[9] T. K. Doty, *Lessons In Holiness* (Canton, Ohio: Published by the Author, 1885), p. 9.

[10] Samuel Chadwick, *The Way to Pentecost* (New York: Fleming H. Revell Co., n.d.), pp. 84, 85.

[11] Joseph Agar Beet, *Holiness: Symbolic and Real* (Cincinnati: Jennings and Graham, 1910), pp. 80, 81.

[12] *The Second Work of Grace,* D. Shelby Corlett, ed. (Kansas City, Mo.: Beacon Hill Press), pp. 39, 41, 93-95.

[13] *Ibid.*, p. 40.

[14] J. Baines Atkinson, *To The Uttermost,* p. 70.

[15] Harald Lindstrom, *Wesley and Sanctification* (New York: Abingdon, n.d.), p. 153. See also John Wesley, "A Plain Account of Christian Perfection" in *Works,* XI: 443; and "Farther Thoughts on Christian Perfection," *Ibid.*, p. 417.

[16] G. Campbell Morgan, *Discipleship* (New York: Fleming H. Revell), p. 14.

[17] Paul S. Rees, Article in *"The Pentecostal Herald,"* published at Louisville, Ky.

[18] Author unknown.

[19] R. Barclay Warren's Thesis for the Bachelor of Divinity degree, Immanuel College, Victoria University, Toronto, Canada, p. 20.

[20] *The Second Work of Grace,* p. 40. (See Note 12 above.)

Notes To Chapter Three

[1] John Wesley, *The Works of the Rev. John Wesley,* (Third edition, Complete and Unabridged. Reprint edition. Kansas City, Mo.: Beacon Hill Press, 1978), XII: 225. Note: All references to Wesley's *Works* throughout this book are to this edition.

[2] S. M. Merrill, *Aspects of Christian Experience* (Cincinnati: Curtis and Jennings, 1882), p. 262.

[3] Barry, *Meditations on the Office and Work of the Holy Spirit.*

[4] Samuel Wakefield, *A Complete System of Christian Theology* (Cincinnati: Curtis and Jennings, 1869), pp. 167, 168.

[5] Luther Lee, *Elements of Theology, or An Exposition of the Origin, Doctrines, Morals and Institutions of Christianity* (Syracuse, N.Y.: A. W. Hall, Agent, 1899), pp. 76, 77.

[6] W. N. Clarke, *An Outline of Christian Theology* (New York: Scribner and Sons, n.d.), pp. 89-93.

[7] Joseph Agar Beet, *Holiness: Symbolic and Real* (Cincinnati: Jennings and Graham, 1910), p. 28.

[8] *Ibid.,* p. 51.

[9] Augustus H. Strong, *Systematic Theology* (Philadephia: Judson Press, 1907), "Preface," p. x.

[10] *Ibid.,* p. 266.

[11] *Ibid.,* p. 268.

[12] *Ibid.,* p. 264.

[13] H. Orton Wiley, *Systematic Theology* (Kansas City, Mo.: Beacon Hill Press, 1940), II: 354.

[14] *Ibid.,* p. 365.

[15] *Ibid.*

[16] John McClintock and James Strong, eds., *Cyclopedia of Biblical, Theological and Ecclesiastical Literature* (New York: Harper and Brothers, 1891, 12 vols.), IV: 296.

[17] S. M. Merrill, *op. cit.,* p. 263.

[18] R. S. Foster, *Philosophy of Christian Experience* (New York: Hunt and Eaton, 1891), pp. 168, 169.

[19]G. Campbell Morgan, *The Crises of the Christ* (New York: Fleming H. Revell, 1903), p. 440.

[20]Samuel Wakefield, *op. cit.*, p. 170.

[21]R. S. Foster, *op. cit.*, p. 169.

[22]*The Second Work of Grace*, D. Shelby Corlett, ed. (Kansas City, Mo.: Beacon Hill Press. n.d.), p. 106.

[23]*Ibid.*, p. 56.

Notes To Chapter Four

[1] Arthur W. Pink, *The Doctrine of Sanctification* (Grand Rapids, Mich.: Baker Book House, 1965), p. 9.

[2] *Ibid.,* p. 41.

[3] *Ibid.,* p. 8.

[4] *Webster's Second New International Dictionary,* Unabridged edition, (Springfield, Mass., G. and C. Merriam Co.).

[5] R. D. Shaw, *The Pauline Epistles,* p. 232.

[6] Augustus H. Strong, *Systematic Theology* (Philadelphia: Judson Press, 1907), p. 881.

[7] Oswald Chambers, *The Philosophy of Sin,* pp. 28, 29, 39.

[8] John McClintock and James Strong, eds., *Cyclopedia of Biblical, Theological and Ecclesiastical Literature* (New York: Harper and Brothers, 1891), IX: 331.

[9] Nelson, *Sin and Salvation,* p. 91.

[10] H. M. Mallalieu, *The Fullness of the Blessing of the Gospel of Christ* (New York: Eaton and Mains, 1903), p. 11.

[11] H. Orton Wiley, *Systematic Theology* (Kansas City, Mo.: Beacon Hill Press, 1940), II: 358.

[12] Andrew Johnson, *Twelve Striking Sermons* (Louisville, Ky.: Pentecostal Publishing Company, 1918), p. 44.

[13] L. D. McCabe, *Light on the Pathway of Holiness* (New York: Phillips and Hunt, n.d.), p. 63.

[14] *Ibid.*

[15] Thomas Cook, *New Testament Holiness* (London: Epworth Press, 1948), p. 33.

[16] J. Baines Atkinson, *To the Uttermost,* pp. 68, 69.

[17] Henry C. Sheldon, *A System of Christian Doctrine* (Cincinnati: Jennings and Graham, 1903), pp. 464, 465.

[18] John Wesley, *Works,* (See Note 1, Chapter 3), XI: 393, 441, 442.

[19] L. D. McCabe, *op. cit.,* p. 58.

[20] Harold Paul Sloan, *Not Disobedient Unto the Heavenly Vision,* pp. 30, 31. Used by permission.

[21]*Ibid.,* p. 54.

[22]John Wesley, *Works,* (See Note 1, Chapter 3), VIII: 47.

[23]Harold Paul Sloan, *op. cit.,* pp. 51, 52.

[24]R. S. Foster, *The Philosophy of Christian Experience.* (New York: Hunt and Eaton, 1891), pp. 161-163.

[25]Ruth Paxon Hood, *Life on the Highest Plane,* Three volumes bound together, (Chicago: Moody Press, n.d.), III: 16, 18.

[26]Henry C. Sheldon, *op. cit.,* p. 468.

Notes To Chapter Five

[1] Isaiah Reid, *How They Grow* (Chicago: Christian Witness Co.), pp. 10, 11.

[2] Charles P. Masden, *Pentecost in Practical Life,* pp. 88-90.

[3] J. Paul Taylor, *The Music of Pentecost* (Winona Lake, Ind.: Light and Life Press, 1951), p. 67.

[4] Hilary T. Hudson, *The Methodist Armor* (Nashville: M. E. Church, 1891), p. 109.

[5] T. M. Anderson, *After Sanctification What?* (Kansas City, Mo.: Nazarene Pub. House, 1929), p. 12.

[6] *Ibid.,* p. 15.

[7] Charles O. Eldredge, *Methodist Theology* (Reprint edition, Salem, Ohio: Schmul Publishing Co.), p. 26.

[8] Thomas Cook, *New Testament Holiness* (London: Epworth Press, 1948).

[9] Harald Lindstrom, *Wesley and Sanctification* (London: Epworth Press), p. 141.

[10] E. H. Sugden, *The Standard Sermons of the Rev. John Wesley,* edited and annotated, 4th edition (London: Epworth Press), II: 156.

[11] *Ibid.*

[12] John Telford, ed., *The Letters of the Rev. John Wesley* (London: Epworth Press, 1931. 8 vols.), VI: 142.

[13] L. D. McCabe, *Light on the Pathway of Holiness* (New York: Phillips and Hunt), p. 89.

[14] Wilson T. Hogue, An Editorial in "The Free Methodist."

[15] G. P. Pardington, *The Crisis of the Deeper Life* (Harrisburg, Pa.: Christian Publications), p. 124.

[16] Albert Barnes, *Notes on the New Testament* (Grand Rapids, Mich.: Baker Book House), *in loc.*

[17] John Wesley, *Explanatory Notes Upon the New Testament* (Cincinnati: Hitchcock and Walden, n.d.), *in loc.*

[18] Adam Clarke, *Commentary on the New Testament* (Nashville: Abingdon, n.d.), *in loc.*

[19] John Wesley, *Works,* (See Note 1, Chapter 3), *in loc.*

[20] Albert Barnes, *op. cited., in loc.*

[21] *Ibid.*

[22] *The Pulpit Commentary,* H. D. M. Spence, ed. (Grand Rapids, Mich.: Wm. b. Eerdman, 1950), *in loc.*

[23] Adam Clarke, *op cit., in loc.*

[24] Daniel Steele, *Half-Hours With St. Paul* (Salem, Ohio: Schmul Publishing Co., reprint edition), pp. 113, 114.

[25] William Jones, *Entire Sanctification* (Philadelphia: National Publishing Association for the Promotion of Holiness, n.d.), pp. 184-187.

[26] Daniel Whedon, *Whedon's Commentary* (New York: Eaton and Mains, 1875), *in loc.*

[27] Harry M. Ironside, *Notes on Philippians* (New York: Loizeaux Brothers), *in loc.*

[28] L. D. McCabe, *op. cit.,* p. 12.

[29] H. Orton Wiley, *Systematic Theology* (Kansas City, Mo.: Beacon Hill Press, 1940), II: 354.

[30] Jonathan Dungan, *The King's Standard* (New York: The Methodist Book Concern, n.d.), pp. 119-122.

[31] Harald Lindstrom, *op. cit.,* p. 103.

[32] *Ibid.,* p. 105.

[33] John Wesley, *Works,* VIII: 177. (See Note 1, Chapter 3).

[34] Harald Lindstrom, *op. cit.,* 119.

[35] *Ibid.,* pp. 123-125.

[36] H. M. Mallalieu, *The Fullness of the Blessing* (New York: Eaton and Mains, 1903), pp. 154-156.

[37] Barry, *Meditations on the Office and Work of the Holy Spirit,* pp. 145, 146.

Notes To Chapter Six

[1] Sheridan Baker, *The Hidden Manna* (Chicago: The Christian Witness Co., n.d.), pp. 67, 68.

[2] R. S. Foster, *The Philosophy of Christian Experience* (New York: Hunt and Eaton, 1891), pp. 134, 135.

[3] *Ibid.*, p. 135.

[4] *Ibid.*

[5] Sheridan Baker, *op. cit.*, p. 69.

[6] Asbury Lowery, *Possibilities of Grace* (Chicago: The Christian Witness Co.), pp. 29, 30.

[7] S. M. Merrill, *Aspects of Christian Experience* (Cincinnati: Curtis and Jennings, 1882), pp. 263, 264.

[8] L. D. McCabe, *Light on the Pathway of Holiness* (New York: Phillips and Hunt), pp. 76, 77.

[9] George A. Buttrick, *So We Believe, So We Pray.*

[10] Joseph Agar Beet, *Holiness: Symbolic and Real* (Cincinnati: Jennings and Graham, 1910), p. 108.

[11] *Ibid.*, p. 117.

[12] Joe Brice, *Pentecost (Salem, Ohio: Schmul Publishing Company, reprint edition, 1974), p. 112.*

[13] J. A. Broadbelt, *Full Salvation* (London: Marshall, Morgan and Scott, n.d.), p. 52.

[14] George D. Watson, *The Secret of Spiritual Power* (Cincinnati, Ohio: God's Bible School, n.d.), pp. 132, 133.

[15] Joe Brice, *op. cit.*, p. 70.

Notes To Chapter Seven

[1] J. Baines Atkinson, *To The Uttermost*, p. 68.

[2] William Jones, *Entire Sanctification* (Philadelphia: National Publishing Association for the Promotion of Holiness), p. 107.

[3] *Ibid.*

[4] W. N. Clarke, *Outline of Christian Theology* (New York: Scribner and Sons, n.d.), p. 199.

[5] Jonathon Dungan, *The King's Standard* (New York: The Methodist Book Concern).

[6] Luther Lee, *Elements of Divinity, or An Exposition of the Origin, Doctrines, and Morals and Institutions of Christianity* (Syracuse, New York: A. W. Hall, 1899), pp. 76, 77.

[7] W. N. Clarke, *op. cit.*, p. 102.

[8] H. L. Goudge, *Commentary on I Corinthians*, pp. 87, 88.

[9] R. S. Foster, quoted in Leewin B. Williams, *Holiness Illustrations*.

Notes To Chapter Eight

[1]Josephus Stephan, *Four D's After Sanctification* (Louisville, Ky.: Pickett Publishing Co., 1893), p. 11.

[2]Harry E. Jessop, *The Heritage of Holiness* (Kansas City, Mo.: Beacon Hill Press, n.d.), p. 25.

[3]A. W. Tozer, *The Pursuit of God* (Harrisburg, Pa.: Christian Publications), p. 8.

[4]*Ibid.*, pp. 12, 13.

[5]Chester E. Tulga, *The Doctrine of Holiness In These Times* (Second Edition, Little Rock, Ark.: The Challenger Press, 1976), pp. 8, 13-20.

[6]J. Stephan, *op. cit.*, pp. 19, 20.

[7]*Ibid.*, p. 20.

[8]*Ibid.*, p. 21.

[9]*Ibid.*, p. 22.

[10]Foreman Lincicome, *The Three D's of the Sanctified* (3rd edition, Winona Lake, Ind.: Light and Life Press, 1932), p. 25.

[11]Martin Wells Knapp, *Impressions From Above and Below, How to Test Them* (Cincinnati, Ohio: Revivalist Publishing House, 1892).

[12]Leon Chambers and Mildred Chambers, *Human Nature and Perfecting Holiness* (Fairfax, Alabama: Leon Chambers, 1972).

[13]F. Lincicome, *op. cit.*, p. 7.

[14]*Ibid.*, pp. 9, 10.

[15]*Ibid.*, p. 7.

[16]Adam Clarke, *Christian Theology* (Reprint edition, Salem, Ohio: Convention Book Store, 1967), p. 192.

[17]Lincicome, *op. cit.*, p. 19.

[18]L. R. Dunn, *Holiness to the Lord* (New York: Nelson and Phillips, 1874), pp. 42, 43.

[19]Lewis T. Corlett, *Holiness the Harmonizing Experience* (Kansas City, Mo.: Beacon Hill Press, 1951), p. 6.

[20]Josephus Stephan, *op. cit.*, p. 49.

[21]*Ibid.*, p. 51.

[22] Clyde M. Narramore, *Perfectionism . . . Its Causes and Cures* (Rosemead, California: Narramore Christian Foundation, 1979).

[23] Don Bastian, Leslie R. Marston, Editors, *Thumbnail Sketches of Doctrinal Patterns* (A Leaflet, Winona Lake, Ind.: Forward Movement, Free Methodist headquarters, n.d.).

[24] *Ibid.*

[25] *Ibid.*

[26] T. M. Anderson, *After Sanctification* (Third printing, Circleville, Ohio: Advocate Publishing House, 1961); Daniel Steele, *Milestone Papers on Christian Progress* (Salem, Ohio: Schmul Publishers, reprint edition, 1976), esp. Part II, pp. 171-222; Keith Drury, *Holiness for Ordinary People* (Marion, Ind.: The Wesley Press, 1983), pp. 67-81, 119-126.

[27] Stephan, *op. cit.*, pp. 46, 47.

[28] John R. Church, *Is God Responsible for My Temptations?* (Louisville, Ky.: Herald Press, n.d.), pp. 40-55.

[29] Leon Chambers, Mildred Chambers, *op. cit.*, pp. 27-29.

[30] Adam Clarke, *op. cit., pp. 347-50.* See also Daniel Steele, *Milestone Papers . . .* (Note 26), pp. 133-136.

[31] John Findlater, *Perfect Love, A Study of John Wesley's View of the Ideal Christian Life (Reprint edition, Salem, Ohio: Schmul Publishing Co., Inc., 1985), pp. 174, 175.*

[32] W. E. Vine, *An Expository Dictionary of the New Testament Words* (Old Tappan, N. J.: Fleming H. Revell Company, 17th impression, 1966).

[33] Harry E. Jessop, *Foundation of Doctrine* (University Park, Iowa: Vennard College, 13th printing, 1974), p. 125.

[34] John Wesley, *The Works of John Wesley* (Third Edition, Complete and Unabridged, Kansas City, Mo.: Beacon Hill Press of Kansas City, 1978), vol. VI: 412, 413.

[35] *Ibid.*, VI: 477, 478.

[36] *Ibid.*, VI: 479.

[37] Daniel Steele, *Steele's Answers* (Chicago: The Christian Witness Co.), p. 134.

[38] Daniel Steele, *Milestone Papers . . .* (Salem, Ohio: Schmul Publishers, reprint edition, n.d.), Chapters VII and XIX.

[39] *Ibid.*, pp. 38, 39.

[40]*Ibid.,* p. 39.
[41]*Ibid.*
[42]*Ibid.*
[43]*Ibid.,* p. 40.
[44]John Wesley, *Works,* XIII: 394.
[45]Daniel Steele, *Milestone Papers,* pp. 42-43.
[46]John Wesley, *Works,* XI: 396, 397.

Notes To Chapter Nine

[1] John Wesley, *The Works of John Wesley, Third London edition, Complete and Unabridged* (London: Mason, 1830. 14 vols.) IX: 22, 29. All references to Wesley's *Works* in this chapter are to that edition.

[2] T. B. Neely, *Doctrinal Standards of Methodism* (New York, Fleming H. Revell, 1918), p. 274.

[3] Sydney B. Dimon, *The Psychology of the Methodist Revival* (Nashville: Whittemore and Smith, 1926), p. 242.

[4] John Wesley, *Works*, IV: 445. (See Note 1.)

[5] John Telford, ed., *The Letters of John Wesley*, Standard Edition (London: Epworth Press, 1931), VIII: 238.

[6] *Ibid.*, p. 241.

[7] John Telford, *op. cit.*, VI: 116.

[8] J. R. Green, *A Short History of the English People*, revised edition (New York: Harper and Brothers, 1898), Chapters 9 and 10.

[9] J. S. Simon, *John Wesley and the Religious Societies* (London: Epworth Press, 1921).

[10] John H. Overton, *The Evangelical Revival of the Eighteenth Century* (New York: A. D. F. Randolph, 1886), p. 4.

[11] *Ibid.*, p. 6.

[12] See President Little's brochure, "*John Wesley, Preacher of Scriptural Christianity,*" copyrighted by the author 1903, for a description of conditions at Oxford and the sermon which separated Wesley from Oxford University, pp. 12-15.

[13] George Peck, *The Scriptural Doctrine of Christian Perfection* (New York: Lane and Sandford, 1842), pp. 199, 200.

[14] J. H. Whiteley, *Wesley's England* (London: Epworth Press, 1938).

[15] *Ibid.*, pp. 221, 224, 226.

[16] Luke Tyerman, *The Life and Times of the Rev. John Wesley* (New York: Harper and Brothers, 1872. 3 volumes), II: 598.

[17] E. H. Sugden, ed., *The Standard Sermons of John Wesley, Annotated.* Introduction to Sermon XXXV on Christian Perfection (London: Epworth Press, 4th Annotated edition).

[18] Edwin D. Mouzon, *Fundamentals of Methodism* (Nashville: Lamar and Barton, 1924), p. 8.

[19] *Ibid.*, p. 68.

[20] J. S. Simon, *John Wesley, the Master Builder* (London: Epworth Press, 1927).

[21] R. Newton Flew, *The Idea of Christian Perfection in Christian Theology* (New York: Humanities Press, Inc., 1968. First published 1934), p. 323.

[22] *Ibid.*, pp. 329, 330.

[23] Maxim Piette, *John Wesley in the Evolution of Protestantism* (New York: Sheed and Ward, 1937), p. 443.

[24] John Wesley, *Works*, VI: 411-424. (See Note 1.)

[25] Frances J. McConnell, *The Essentials of Methodism* (New York: The Methodist Book Concern, 1916), p. 21.

[26] F. J. McConnell, *John Wesley* (New York: The Abingdon Press, 1939), p. 314. Used by permission of copyright owner.

[27] William E. Sangster, *The Path to Perfection* (Nashville: Abingdon-Cokesbury Press), pp. 142, 143.

[28] John M. Moore, *Methodism in Belief and Action* (New York: Abingdon-Cokesbury, 1946), pp. 51, 52. Used by permission.

[29] Samuel Chadwick, *The Call to Christian Perfection* (London: Epworth Press, 1936), p. 9.

[30] John Wesley, *Works*, XI: 398. (See Note 1.)

[31] *Ibid.*, V: 204, 215.

[32] *Ibid.*, XI: 396, 418; see also V: 90; XI: 280.

[33] See J. A. Wood, *Christian Perfection As Taught by John Wesley* (Boston: McDonald and Gill, 1885).

[34] John Telford, ed., *op. cit.*, V: 25-27. (See Note 5.)

[35] Maxim Piette, *op. cit.*, p. 436.

[36] T. B. Neely, *op. cit.*, p. 273. (See Note 2.)

[37] John Wesley, *Works*, I: 476.

[38] *Ibid.*, XI: 369. (See the Editor of the Third London edition's Note on the dates of revision of "The Plain Account of Christian Perfection" in *Works*, XI: 366.)

[39] *Ibid.*, XI: 383-385.

[40] William Myles, *A Chronological Review of the People*

Called Methodists (4th edition, London: Thos. Cordeux, Agent, 1813), p. 84.

[41] John Wesley, *Works,* XI: 446.

[42] John Telford, ed., *op. cit.,* V: 16.

[43] William Myles, *op. cit.,* p. 124f.

[44] John Telford, *op. cit.,* VIII: 190.

[45] For a detailed study of Wesley's views on sanctification as a part of the process of salvation, see Harald Lindstrom's *Wesley and Sanctification: A Study in the Doctrine of Salvation* (London: Epworth Press).

[46] E. H. Sugden, ed., *op. cit.,* II: 445.

[47] *Ibid.,* p. 448.

[48] John Wesley, *Works,* XI: 401.

[49] E. H. Sugden, ed., *op. cit.,* II: 451, 457, 458.

[50] G. Eayrs, *John Wesley, Christian Philosopher and Church Founder* (London: Epworth Press, 1926), p. 160.

[51] This letter, too long to quote in this article, may be found in Tyerman's *Life and Times of John Wesley* (See Note 16) II: 597, 598; and in *The Journal of John Wesley,* Standard Edition, edited by Nehemiah Curnock (Note 55 below) in II: 197, 198; and in Telford's edition of *The Letters of the Rev. John Wesley,* V: 43, 44. (See Note 5 above.)

[52] John Wesley, *Works,* XI: 419.

[53] John Telford, ed., *op. cit.,* III: 168.

[54] *Ibid.,* V: 25, 26.

[55] Nehemiah Curnock, *The Journals of John Wesley* (London: Epworth Press, 1938, 8 vols.), III: 42.

[56] Luke Tyerman, *op. cit.,* III: 13.

[57] John Wesley, *Works,* XI: 398.

[58] *Ibid.,* XI: 419, 420.

[59] E. H. Sugden, ed., *op. cit.,* II: 453.

[60] John Telford, ed., *op. cit.,* V: 258, 259.

[61] John Wesley, *Works,* III: 161.

[62] William Myles, *op. cit.,* p. 87.

[63] John Telford, ed., *op. cit.,* IV: 192.

[64] Nehemiah Curnock, ed., *op. cit.,* III: 157.

[65]Olin A. Curtis, *The Christian Faith* (New York: Eaton and Mains, 1905), p. 376. Used by Permission.

[66]L. R. Marston, ed., *The Wesleyan Message,* A Compilation of Addresses by representatives of the Free Methodist Church (Winona Lake, Ind.: Light and Life Press, 1940), p. 132.

[67]"Wesleyan Methodist Magazine," 1867, pp. 23-30.

[68]W. F. Mallalieu, quoted by J. A. Wood, *Christian Perfection as Taught by John Wesley,* (Reprint Edition, Salem, Ohio: Schmul Publishers, n.d.), p. 7.